INTERVIEWING FOR ASSESSMENT

A PRACTICAL GUIDE FOR SCHOOL PSYCHOLOGISTS AND SCHOOL COUNSELORS

INTERVIEWING FOR ASSESSMENT

MICHAEL HASS

WILEY

Published by John Wiley & Sons, Inc., Hoboken, New Jersey.
Published simultaneously in Canada.

For general information on our other products and services, please contact our Customer Care Department within the U.S. at 800-956-7739, outside the U.S. at 317-572-3986, or fax 317-572-4002.

Wiley publishes in a variety of print and electronic formats and by print-on-demand. Some material included with standard print versions of this book may not be included in e-books or in print-on-demand. If this book refers to media such as a CD or DVD that is not included in the version you purchased, you may download this material at http://booksupport.wiley.com. For more information about Wiley products, visit www.wiley.com.

Library of Congress Cataloging-in-Publication Data

Names: Hass, Michael R., author.
Title: Interviewing for assessment : a practical guide for school psychologists and school counselors / by Michael Hass.
Description: First edition. | Hoboken, New Jersey : John Wiley & Sons, 2018. | Includes index. |
Identifiers: LCCN 2018001352 (print) | LCCN 2018012415 (ebook) | ISBN 9781119166931 (pdf) | ISBN 9781119166948 (epub) | ISBN 9781119166863 (pbk.)
Subjects: LCSH: Psychological tests for children. | Behavioral assessment of children. | Educational tests and measurements.
Classification: LCC BF722.3 (ebook) | LCC BF722.3 .H37 2018 (print) | DDC 158.3/9—dc23
LC record available at https://lccn.loc.gov/2018001352

Cover Design: Wiley
Cover Illustration: © royaltystockphoto.com/Shutterstock

FIRST EDITION

10 9 8 7 6 5 4 3 2 1

To my students, whose intelligence and desire to serve children, families, and schools inspire me to be the best practitioner, mentor, and teacher I can possibly be.

Contents

Acknowledgments

This is a better book because of the efforts of many people who have supported me and this project along the way. I am forever grateful to my colleagues at Chapman University—Anna Abdou, John Brady, Randy Busse, Jeanne Anne Carriere, Amy Jane Griffiths, Kelly Kennedy, and Hilary Leath—for their humor, companionship, intelligence, and unwavering commitment to our students. They have made so much more possible than I could ever have accomplished on my own.

I am also grateful to the Friends of the Book, who included Zoe Alvarez, Libby Barnish, Margie Curwin, Michael Doria, Sarah Ferrentino, Cynthia Olaya, and Pedro Olvera. They each gave prompt and insightful feedback that helped me stay focused on the goal of making this book as practical and useful as possible.

A big thanks to Patricia Harriman of FinalEyes Editing & Publishing Partners and the support team at John Wiley & Sons, including Darren Lalonde, Monica Rogers, Manish Luthra, and Shandhya Rajan.

Lastly, I am forever grateful to Nury for her support and ability to remind me of what is important when I lose track.

CHAPTER 1

Introduction to Interviewing for Assessment

Kelly is a 10-year-old girl with Down syndrome. She is in a fourth-grade general education classroom with a one-on-one aide. Kelly has received special education services since she was 3 years old and has been evaluated several times. After her last reevaluation, her parents asked for further assessment because, in their words, the last evaluation had not done enough to identify Kelly's strengths and had focused too much on standardized test scores and not enough on her actual performance in the classroom. The report written following the prior evaluation indicated test scores as well as her teacher's general descriptions of her behavior in the classroom.

Purpose and Goals of This Book

Kelly illustrates two points that will be important throughout this book. One is that, although the quantitative data produced by standardized tests and behavior rating scales can be valuable, they cannot by themselves provide a holistic picture of a child. For this, it is necessary to talk with Kelly and the people who know her best—her parents and her teachers—to ask them focused questions and listen well to produce a description of Kelly that is authentic and credible. The second point is that these conversations are not simply in the service of arriving at a diagnosis. No one doubts that Kelly has Down syndrome. In addition, in Kelly's case, no one doubts that she has at least a mild intellectual disability or difficulties expressing herself verbally. This information is easily available to us via scores on standardized tests. What we do not know, aside from these broad brushstrokes, is what her unique strengths and challenges are. My assertion in this book is that the best way to arrive at this knowledge is through interviewing both Kelly and the important adults in her life. My overall goal in writing this book is to assist practitioners in being able to do this with skill and confidence.

Interviewing has long been embraced by mental health professionals as a flexible way of gathering information from the clients they work with. Furthermore, interviewing is so ubiquitous in society at large that we are said to live in what Atkinson and Silverman (1997) called "the interview society." One only has to watch the news on television or pick up a magazine to find interviews being used to deliver information, shed light on issues, or simply unveil the experiences of a popular personality.

The importance of interviewing lies in its flexibility to be used for different purposes. In psychological or educational assessment, it can be used to better understand someone's social and cultural context, clarify clients' concerns, determine a formal classification or diagnosis, and/or gather information important for developing solutions to problems (e.g., Beaver & Busse, 2000; Vacc & Juhnke, 1997; Watkins, Campbell, Nieberding, & Hallmark, 1995). Interviewing is such a pervasive part of what counselors and psychologists are expected to do that, as Whitcomb and Merrell (2013) point out, it has become part of the mystique of being a mental health professional. Although interviewing is not the X-ray superpower laypeople imagine it to be, it is hard to envision a day going by in the lives of counselors or psychologists when they do not gather information from students, parents, or teachers by having conversations with them. This importance is reflected in the quantity of literature available on interviewing. For example, a search of the electronic catalog at the university where I teach, using the term *clinical interviewing* yielded almost 1,300 books and nearly 49,000 journal articles.

Yet despite its presence in the literature and apparent importance as a professional competency, interviewing is often an underutilized part of the assessment process, at least among school-based practitioners. Over the past several years, I have read dozens of psychoeducational evaluation reports and interacted with hundreds of participants in professional development workshops I lead. Although this is certainly limited data, my observation is that, although interviewing has been described as "the hallmark of assessment processes and perhaps the most common method used to obtain information to evaluate individuals" (Busse & Beaver, 2000, p. 235), it seems to take a back seat to other forms of evaluation data such as standardized tests.

At least some research supports this conclusion. For example, the results of a survey of 214 practicing school psychologists found that even with evaluations of children suspected of having the educational classification of Emotional Disturbance, a student interview was one of the most excluded assessment methods (Allen & Hanchon, 2013). This is especially striking given that the focus of evaluations to decide Emotional Disturbance is on social, behavioral, and emotional functioning; this emphasis calls for interviews of children, parents, and teachers.

In part, the underutilization of interviewing may be because interviewing for assessment demands a unique blend of both interpersonal skills and professional knowledge (Sattler, 1998; Whitcomb & Merrell, 2013). For example, to be competent at interviewing requires that practitioners possess knowledge of typical and atypical child development, formal classification systems (e.g., *Diagnostic and Statistical Manual* [*DSM*], American Psychiatric Association, 2013; Individuals with Disabilities Education Improvement Act [IDEIA], 2004; etc.) as well as the communication skills needed to flexibly respond to the demands of persons of different ages, persons with different social and emotional challenges, and persons with varied social and cultural backgrounds. This includes skills for fostering a collaborative relationship and skillful questioning strategies. School-based practitioners must also have a good understanding of learning, curriculum, and pedagogy. This unique combination of skills and knowledge can make interviewing for assessment difficult to learn and practice well.

Nonetheless, skillful interviewing is critical to being an effective school counselor or school psychologist and a fundamental part of the assessment process. Given its importance, the goal of this book is to help students and practitioners learn to be more comfortable and skillful using interviews to gather information from children, parents, and teachers. A secondary goal is for readers to better understand how interviews can be used with other assessment methods as part of a comprehensive assessment.

The ideas discussed here are drawn from my 35 years' experience as a school psychologist and psychotherapist, much of that spent working with children and youth with social, emotional, and behavioral challenges. It also comes from my nearly 20 years as an educator of school counselors and school psychologists and my efforts to better understand and teach the ideas and skills that are now part of this book. The outcome of this experience is several *big ideas* that form the basis of this book and the approach to interviewing that I advocate.

Big Ideas of This Book

Interviewing for Assessment and Intervention, Not Just Diagnosis

Much of the literature on interviewing focuses on clinical interviewing. As Whitcomb and Merrell (2013) point out, the term *clinical interviewing* describes interviewing for the purpose of gathering information about behavioral, social, and emotional functioning in order to better understand problems in these areas. Broadly interpreted, this definition seems appropriate for both clinical and educational settings. Unfortunately, much of the literature on clinical interviewing more narrowly places a premium on accurate diagnosis with the assumption that this will lead to clear treatment recommendations. This logic is derived from the medical model with its emphasis on diagnosis and the close relationship between accurate classification and treatment (Kamphaus, Dowdy, Kim, & Chin, 2013). This approach, when applied to the kinds of human problems that mental health practitioners deal with, has been criticized on both philosophical and practical grounds (e.g., De Jong & Kim Berg, 2013; Kamphaus et al., 2013; Kraemer, 2014; Lopez et al., 2006; Sheridan & Gutkin, 2000).

These critiques, and the strengths and weaknesses of formal diagnoses based on a medical model, will be discussed in more depth in Chapter 8, but what is important for the moment is that these criticisms seem especially salient in school-based practice, where the viewpoint is more ecological and the emphasis is on problem-solving and prevention of problems (Burns, 2011). As Sheridan and Gutkin (2000) state it, "By focusing almost exclusively upon child/pathology-related factors, the medical model leads school psychologists to both ask and answer the wrong questions" (p. 486).

Because of these concerns, I have chosen to use the broader term *interviewing for assessment and intervention* rather than *clinical interviewing*. I start with the assumption that any school-based assessment can serve multiple purposes and that one of these may be to assist in making a determination about the type of problem that someone has. Yet, left here, interviews and assessments in general have limited utility. Chief among the limitations is that diagnoses often have limited clinical validity (Kamphaus et al., 2013). In other words, they do not contribute very much to the development of strategies, programs, or interventions that promote greater success and well-being, which is arguably the most important point of any assessment. Without this, interviews—and the assessments they are part of—are at best of limited value and at worst, hollow technical exercises.

Given the broader perspective of this book, later chapters will focus on the use of assessment interviews for different purposes, such as interviewing to gather background and contextual information, interviewing for strengths and resources, and interviewing to establish next steps and goals in addition to what has been traditionally considered clinical interviewing—that is, interviewing to establish an accurate diagnosis or classification.

Collaboration Is the First Goal of All Interviews

If, as noted earlier, the end goal of an assessment is to gather information that helps in the development of plans or programs that promote greater success and well-being, it is critical that an overarching purpose of any interview is to promote a collaborative working relationship with the interviewee. This is equally true if the person being interviewed is a child, parent, or other professional. In the context of clinical interviewing, this has been called *diagnostic engagement* (Cepeda & Gotanco, 2017), which is linked conceptually to what has been called the *therapeutic alliance* (Horvath, Del Re, Flückiger, & Symonds, 2011). The importance of relationship as a key variable in client change is well established in the literature on counseling and psychotherapy (e.g., Lambert, 2004; Norcross, 2001; Wampold, 2001). Although the focus of this book is not on therapy per se, the relationship between practitioners and clients also has important implications for interviewing for assessment.

As noted previously, the collaborative relationship between a psychotherapist and client has been conceptualized as a *therapeutic alliance* (Horvath et al., 2011). The therapeutic alliance has been described as having three components: (1) interpersonal bonds, (2) agreement on goals, and (3) collaboration on therapeutic tasks (Bordin, 1979, 1994). The first element can be seen as the development of a relationship that consists of mutual respect and trust (Horvath et al., 2011). The second and third elements involve the ability to collaboratively engage in the work of therapy (Hatcher & Barends, 2006). The results of the American Psychological Association Division of Psychotherapy Task Force on Empirically Supported Psychotherapy Relationships describe the relationship between therapeutic alliance and the effectiveness of therapy as *demonstrably effective*, their highest standard for evidence, and suggest that it has value apart from any specific theory or technique (Norcross, 2001).

My assumption is that the process of assessment is in the service of intervention, treatment, or therapy—broadly defined (e.g., later counseling or psychotherapy, educational interventions, behavior support plans, and the like). In other words, assessment is never a stand-alone activity but a step in a process that leads to helpful changes in a child's life. Given the importance of relationship in psychotherapy, I also assume that the odds of success in post-assessment interventions increase if there is a bond between the practitioner and the client and agreement on what is to be done and why. More specifically in the case of interviewing for assessment, I also argue that it is reasonable to assume that the quality and accuracy of the information gathered during an assessment will be improved when practitioners pay attention to the alliance early in the relationship.

If establishing a working relationship or alliance is important to client change, then an important question is, what can the practitioner do to help develop this kind of relationship? The answer to this question can best be explained both as a general stance or attitude toward clients and in terms of specific skills. This stance has been described as one of *not knowing* (Anderson & Goolishian, 1992). The skills that follow from this stance have been described in different ways, including *microskills* (Carkhuff, 2000; Truax & Carkhuff, 1967), *O.A.R.S.* in Motivational Interviewing (Miller & Rollnick, 2013), and *skills for not knowing* (De Jong & Kim Berg, 2013). These skills will be discussed in the context of interviewing for assessment in Chapter 4.

The Insider Perspective Is Important

For many, the judgments made from an interview seem more subjective and less defensible than the hard data of test scores and rating scales. Yet, without the information gained from interviewing, assessments can seem depersonalized and even off-putting to stakeholders such as parents and teachers. I have had the experience of working with many parents whose children had been assessed several times, but they remained dissatisfied because they did not "see" their children in the reports and assessment data.

Interviewing then adds important information about how different stakeholders (e.g., parents, teachers, students themselves) view a situation. This insider perspective not only offers ecological validity for information from other sources such as tests or behavior rating scales; it also helps cultivate the collaborative working relationship discussed earlier. Anthropologists have used the terms *emic* to describe the insider understanding of a phenomenon and the word *etic* to describe the perspective of those who observe a person or group as outsiders and analyze their observations using their own categories and systems of classification (Pelto & Pelto, 1986). Practitioners must balance their outsider, or *etic,* expert knowledge with a deep *emic* understanding of how the people they work with view their situations.

This balanced understanding comes from what the cultural anthropologist Clifford Geertz (1973) referred to as a *thick description,* by which he meant a description of not only a specific behavior, but enough rich contextual information so that the behavior becomes meaningful to an outsider. Although assessment serves multiple purposes, the overarching goal of any assessment is to make the unique strengths and challenges of children more meaningful to their parents, their teachers and other professionals who work with them, and the children themselves. It is also important that those we interview feel the relationship is not one-sided and that they are part of the assessment process. This is impossible without the insider perspective that only interviews can provide.

Focus on the Whole Person: Strengths as Well as Problems

Over the past several years a number of researchers and writers have focused on the notion that it is equally, if not more, important for assessments to account for someone's strengths and resources as for problems and psychopathology (e.g., Cox, 2006; Huebner & Gilman, 2003; Jimerson, Sharkey, Nyborg, & Furlong, 2004; Nickerson & Fishman, 2013). Suldo and Shaffer (2008) argue that psychopathology and wellness make important independent contributions to mental health. This argument is in keeping with evidence that suggests that symptoms, or psychopathology, alone do not account for the level of impairment in people with mental health disorders (Winters, Collett, & Myers, 2004) and that strengths and sources of resilience seem to contribute to positive outcomes more than deficits or risk factors alone (Garmezy, 1993; Werner & Smith, 1992).

The inclusion of strengths and resources in a comprehensive assessment has several advantages. Conversations about strengths facilitate the alliance discussed earlier by encouraging client engagement in the assessment process and subsequent treatment (Epstein, Hertzog, & Reid, 2001). These conversations also encourage practitioners to focus on the enhancement of skills and learning and not just on reducing symptoms or problem behaviors (Epstein et al., 2001; Nickerson & Fishman, 2013). Any approach to interviewing for assessment that does not include strengths and resources will provide a partial and incomplete picture of a child.

The Structure of This Book

The next three chapters set the stage for learning to interview for assessment and intervention by providing an overview of interviewing, detailing specific interviewing strategies, and discussing how to work with children of different developmental statuses and cultures. A separate chapter is devoted to observation during an interview, or what is often called a mental status exam.

The following chapters illustrate different uses of interviewing, including (a) interviewing to understand history and context, (b) interviewing to clarify and classify problems, (c) interviewing about academic performance, (d) interviewing to understand strengths and resources, (e) interviewing in high-risk situations such as crisis or threat, and (f) interviewing to establish motivation and commitment. In addition to a discussion of each of these applications of interviewing, each of these chapters will present a case study and sample interview transcripts to help the reader better understand how these skills look in practice with different clients. The last two chapters focus on communicating the key information from interviews to stakeholders either in conferences or meetings, or in written reports.

Chapter 1 Takeaway Points

- Interviewing is an important but underutilized part of any assessment.
- Interviewing for assessment and intervention is more than establishing a diagnosis or classification.
- Collaboration is the first goal of all interviews and is critical to their success.
- Interviewing provides the emic or insider perspective in assessments.
- Interviewing for assessment should focus on the whole person and include his or her strengths as well as problems.

References

Allen, R. A., & Hanchon, T. A. (2013). What can we learn from school-based emotional disturbance practices? Implications for practice and preparation in school psychology. *Psychology in the Schools, 50*(3), 290–299. doi:10.1002/pits.21671

American Psychiatric Association. (2013). *Diagnostic and statistical manual of mental disorders* (5th ed.). Washington, DC: Author.

Anderson, H., & Goolishian, H. (1992). The client is the expert: A not-knowing approach to therapy. In S. McNamee & K. Gergen (Eds.), *Social construction and the therapeutic process* (pp. 25–39). Newbury Park, CA: Sage.

Atkinson, P., & Silverman, D. (1997). Kundera's "Immortality": The interview society and the invention of the self. *Qualitative Inquiry, 3*, 304–325.

Beaver, B. R., & Busse, R. T. (2000). Informant reports: Conceptual and research bases of interviews with parents and teachers. In E. S. Shapiro & T. R. Kratochwill (Eds.), *Behavioral assessment in schools: Theory, research, and clinical foundations* (2nd ed., pp. 257–287). New York, NY: Guilford Press.

Bordin, E. S. (1979). The generalizability of the psychoanalytic concept of the working alliance. *Psychotherapy: Theory, Research & Practice, 16*(3), 252–260. doi:10.1037/h0085885

Bordin, E. S. (1994). Theory and research on the therapeutic working alliance: New directions. In A. O. Horvath & L. S. Greenberg (Eds.), *The working alliance: Theory, research, and practice* (pp. 13–37). Oxford, England: Wiley.

Burns, M. K. (2011). School psychology research: Combining ecological theory and prevention science. *School Psychology Review, 40*(1), 132–139.

Busse, R. T., & Beaver, B. R. (2000). Informant report: Parent and teacher interviews. In E. S. Shapiro & T. R. Kratochwill (Eds.), *Conducting school-based assessments of child and adolescent behavior* (pp. 235–273). New York, NY: Guilford Press.

Carkhuff, R. R. (2000). *The art of helping in the 21st century* (8th ed.). Amherst, MA: Human Resource Development Press.

Cepeda, C., & Gotanco, L. (2017). *Psychiatric interview of children and adolescents*. Arlington, VA: American Psychiatric Association.

Cox, K. F. (2006). Investigating the impact of strength-based assessment on youth with emotional or behavioural disorders. *Journal of Child and Family Studies, 15*, 287–301.

De Jong, P., & Kim Berg, I. (2013). *Interviewing for solutions*. Belmont, CA: Brooks/Cole, Cengage Learning.

Epstein, M. H., Hertzog, M. A., & Reid, R. (2001). The Behavioral and Emotional Rating Scale: Long term test–retest reliability. *Behavioral Disorders, 26*(4), 314.

Garmezy, N. (1993). Children in poverty: Resilience despite risk. *Psychiatry, 56*, 127–136.

Geertz, C. (1973). *The interpretation of cultures: Selected essays by Clifford Geertz*. New York, NY: Basic Books.

Hatcher, R. L., & Barends, A. W. (2006). How a return to theory could help alliance research. *Psychotherapy: Theory, Research, Practice, Training, 43*(3), 292–299. doi:10.1037/0033-3204.43.3.292

References

Horvath, A. O., Del Re, A. C., Flückiger, C., & Symonds, D. (2011). Alliance in individual psychotherapy. *Psychotherapy, 48*(1), 9–16. doi:10.1037/a0022186

Huebner, E. S., & Gilman, R. (2003). Toward a focus on positive psychology in school psychology. *School Psychology Quarterly, 18*, 99–102.

Individuals with Disabilities Education Improvement Act, Pub. L. No. 108-446, 118 Stat. 2647 (2004).

Jimerson, S., Sharkey, J., Nyborg, V., & Furlong, M. (2004). Strength-based assessment and school psychology: A summary and synthesis. *The California School Psychologist, 9*, 9–19.

Kamphaus, R. W., Dowdy, E., Kim, S., & Chin, J. (2013). Diagnosis, classification, and screening systems. In D. H. Saklofske, C. R. Reynolds, & V. L. Schwean (Eds.), *The Oxford handbook of child psychological assessment* (pp. 182–201). doi:10.1093/oxfordhb/9780199796304.013.0009

Kraemer, H. C. (2014). The reliability of clinical diagnoses: State of the art. *Annual Review of Clinical Psychology, 10*, 111–130. doi:10.1146/annurev-clinpsy-032813-153739

Lambert, M. (2004). The efficacy and effectiveness of psychotherapy. In M. J. Lambert (Ed.), *Bergin and Garfield's handbook of psychotherapy and behavior change* (5th ed., pp. 139–193). New York, NY: Wiley.

Lopez, S. J., Edwards, L. M., Pedrotti, J. T., Prosser, E. C., LaRue, S., Spalitto, S. V., & Ulven, J. C. (2006). Beyond the DSM-IV: Assumptions, alternatives, and alterations. *Journal of Counseling & Development, 84*(3), 259–267. doi:10.1002/j.1556-6678.2006.tb00404.x

Miller, W. R., & Rollnick, S. (2013). *Motivational interviewing: Helping people change.* New York, NY: Guilford Press.

Nickerson, A. B., & Fishman, C. E. (2013). Promoting mental health and resilience through strength-based assessment in US schools. *Educational and Child Psychology, 30*(4), 7–1.

Norcross, J. C. (Ed.). (2001). Empirically supported therapy relationships: Summary report of the Division 29 Task Force. *Psychotherapy, 38*(4).

Pelto, P. J., & G. H. Pelto (1986). *Anthropological research: The structure of inquiry*. Cambridge, England: Cambridge University Press.

Sattler, J. M. (1998). *Clinical and forensic interviewing of children and families*. San Diego, CA: Author.

Sheridan, S. M., & Gutkin, T. B. (2000). The ecology of school psychology: Examining and changing our paradigm for the 21st century. *School Psychology Review, 29*(4), 485–502.

Suldo, S. M., & Shaffer, E. J. (2008). Looking beyond psychopathology: The dual-factor model of mental health in youth. *School Psychology Review, 37*, 52–68.

Truax, C. B., & Carkhuff, R. R. (1967). *Toward effective counseling and psychotherapy: Training and practice*. Chicago, IL: Aldine.

Vacc, N. A., & Juhnke, G. A. (1997). The use of structured clinical interviews for assessment in counseling. *Journal of Counseling and Development, 75*(6), 470–480.

Wampold, B. E. (2001). *The great psychotherapy debate: Models, methods, and findings*. Mahwah, NJ: Erlbaum.

Watkins, C. J., Campbell, V. L., Nieberding, R., & Hallmark, R. (1995). Contemporary practice of psychological assessment by clinical psychologists. *Professional Psychology, Research and Practice, 26*(1), 54–60.

Werner, E. E., & Smith, R. S. (1992). *Overcoming the odds: High risk children from birth to adulthood*. Ithaca, NY: Cornell University Press.

Whitcomb, S. A., & Merrell, K. W. (2013). *Behavioral, social, and emotional assessment of children and adolescents* (4th ed.). New York, NY: Routledge.

Winters, N. C., Collett, B. R., & Myers, K. (2004). Ten-year review of rating scales, VII: Scales assessing functional impairment. *Journal of the American Academy of Child and Adolescent Psychiatry, 44*(4), 309–338. doi:10.1097/01.chi.0000153230.57344.cd

CHAPTER 2

Interviews as Part of a Comprehensive Assessment

Assessment is an important activity for both school psychologists and school counselors. In the standards of the Council for Accreditation of Counseling and Related Educational Programs (CACREP), assessment is one of the eight core competencies required of counselor education programs at both the masters and doctoral level (CACREP, 2015). The National Association for School Psychologists' (NASP) *A Blueprint for Training and Practice III* highlights the core competency of data-based decision-making (Ysseldyke et al., 2006). NASP also advocates for assessment to be conceptualized as part of a problem-solving process that connects directly to prevention and intervention rather than as a stand-alone activity.

In general, assessment can be defined as the process of gathering information to inform decisions (Salvia, Ysseldyke, & Bolt, 2007). However, prior to deciding what information needs to be gathered or what decisions need to be made, it is important to understand what questions are being posed by the stakeholders who ask for the assessment. From this perspective, assessments are always question driven (Hass & Carriere, 2013). To answer these questions fully and make thoughtful decisions about recommendations that would promote academic success or improve well-being, it is important that assessments be comprehensive. In the context of assessment, the term *comprehensive* and its synonyms such as *complete, broad,* and *inclusive* have theoretical, practical, and legal implications. These different perspectives are important in understanding the role of interviews in assessment.

AN ECOLOGICAL PERSPECTIVE

A comprehensive assessment takes a broad ecological perspective rather than focusing only on individual characteristics (Gutkin, 2012). Building on the work of Bronfenbrenner (1977), an ecological approach to assessment emphasizes the transactional nature of human development and the quality of the relationships between children and their social and physical environments. Brofenbrenner described four social structures that make up the major facets of a child's environment (1977). The *microsystem* is composed of the person and his or her immediate environment, for example, home, school, family, workplace, and so on. The *mesosystem* is the system of connections among the various microsystems in a child's life. This might include home–school communication or links between school and community agencies. The *ecosystem* includes social and cultural structures that do not necessarily have the same immediate impact on children as microsystems but exert their influence more indirectly. These might include social media, government agencies, local systems of transportation, and social networks outside the family. Lastly, the *macrosystem* is the network of larger institutional, cultural, economic, or legal structures of a society. Examples of elements of the macrosystem include laws governing education, economic conditions that influence employment, or the regulations concerning access to health care.

An ecological perspective gives us a wider lens through which to view children and their struggles to be successful in school. This wider lens helps practitioners move away from the limitation of focusing only on within-the-individual variables such as psychopathology or disorders that rarely provide sufficient information to develop effective interventions (Gutkin, 2012). It is important to have an understanding and appreciation of all levels of Bronfenbrenner's four systems (1977). For example, although the *macrosystem* is typically not seen as within the purview of counselors and psychologists, appreciating that personal problems always arise in the context of broader social problems, even if those connections are not obvious, is critical to grasping the entirety of a child's difficulties and struggles to overcome those difficulties (Mills, 1959).

That said, it is the *microsystem* and the *mesosystem* that are most directly accessible as part of a comprehensive assessment. For example, as part of interviews with students, parents, and teachers, practitioners can focus their attention on the quality of the relationships between teacher and student or parent and teacher. It is also important to investigate the classroom instructional environment to better understand what elements can be changed to promote better learning for an individual student (Ysseldyke & Christenson, 2002). The goal of any intervention is often less about "curing" children than about making the systems that affect children's lives work better (Apter & Conoley, 1984).

Ethical and Legal

Looking at assessment from an ecological perspective allows us to better meet the federal laws and regulations that mandate that evaluations to determine if a child has an educational disability be comprehensive (Individuals with Disabilities Education Improvement Act [IDEIA], 2004). This mandate can be divided into two parts. The first says it is necessary to assess in all areas of suspected disability, and the second states it is necessary to assess in all areas of related need (Hass & Carriere, 2013). These are related but distinct mandates. The first is related to the criteria for disability categories in IDEA, for example, specific learning disability, autism, and so on. The second focuses on unique areas of need that may or may not be directly related to the definition of the disability.

To illustrate the difference, let's consider the legal definition of autism for special education purposes:

> Autism means a developmental disability significantly affecting verbal and nonverbal communication and social interaction, generally evident before age three, that adversely affects a child's educational performance. Other characteristics often associated with autism are engagement in repetitive activities and stereotyped movements, resistance to environmental change or change in daily routines, and unusual responses to sensory experiences. (Assistance to States for Education of Children with Disabilities Program and the Preschool Grants for Children with Disabilities Program, CFR Sec. 300.8(c)(1)(i), 2006)

Of course, under this mandate we would have the legal (and practical) obligation to consider the areas of communication and social interaction, sensory experiences, repetitive and stereotyped movements, and resistance to change. At the same time, children with autism often have difficulties in other areas such as self-care or organization of their school materials. The second legal mandate of assessing in all areas of related need would compels us to also assess in these other areas as well as domains directly related to the diagnosis of autism.

These legal mandates compel us to spend time up front in the assessment process to determine what these suspected disabilities and needs are. The data needed to determine the focus of the evaluation come from two sources. One is record review. School records can provide information such as test scores, benchmarks indicating progress toward district academic standards, vision and hearing screening, or office referrals. The second source of data comes from interviews of students, parents, and teachers about what concerns drive the referral for an evaluation (Hass & Carriere, 2013).

Interviewing teachers and parents about their perceptions of children's problems can help practitioners frame the problem and develop hypotheses about the suspected educational disability (i.e., What IDEIA disability categories are suspected in this situation?) and areas of need (i.e., What areas of functioning are of most concern for this child, even if not part of identifying the disability?). Both records and interviews are valuable in meeting the legal mandate for a comprehensive assessment but as Hass and Carriere put it, "the 'soft' data of consumers' concerns expressed in their own terms helps us understand the problem in the context of a particular classroom or family" (2013, p. 20).

FOLLOW STANDARDS OF ACCEPTED PROFESSIONAL PRACTICE

All professions have some sense of what is considered best practice, although the notion of "best" can be controversial and hotly debated. Best practice in framing a comprehensive assessment can be understood using several different models. One approach to understanding this is the acronym R.I.O.T., or (a) *record review,* (b) *interviews,* (c) *observations,* and (d) *tests* or sometimes standardized behavior rating scales (Leung, 1993). Merrell suggests a complementary metric for judging the comprehensiveness of an assessment with the *rule of two* (Merrell, 2008). Like R.I.O.T., the *rule of two* focuses on the principle that a comprehensive assessment must gather information using different *methods* but goes on to suggest that it should also include information from two different *settings* and from different *informants*. The *rule of two* suggests that a reasonable standard for judging sufficient evidence would be two methods, two informants, and two settings. In their discussion of a social-emotional assessment of bilingual/bicultural youth (Table 2.1), Hass and Kennedy (2013) propose a matrix that combines these two approaches.

Practitioners who work in clinical rather than school settings understand the components of a comprehensive assessment through the lens of *case formulation*. Unlike the preceding practice models, models of case formulation are often more explicitly linked to the process

Table 2.1 Matrix for a Comprehensive Social and Emotional Assessment

Informant	Record Review/History	Interview	Observation	Test/Rating Scale
Student				
Teacher				
Parent				
Assessor				
Other				

of determining a diagnosis and the creation of plans for treatment or intervention. For example, Wilmshurst's (2015) three-part approach to case formulation includes (1) problem identification (clarification of problem and diagnosis or classification); (2) problem understanding (factors that precipitate and maintain the problem); and (3) formulation of an intervention plan.

Clinical case formulation can also have a more explicit theoretical orientation than R.I.O.T. or the rule of two. For example, it is possible to look at children and their situations from a biological, behavioral, cognitive behavioral, psychodynamic, or family systems perspective (Wilmshurst, 2015). Wilmshurst argues that Bronfenbrenner's ecological model of development, with its emphasis on understanding how different aspects of a child's environment interact to influence behavior, provides an important framework for integrating the perspectives of other, narrower, theories, such as the ones presented earlier, which often focus on only one aspect of a child's environment or functioning. For example, looking at family roles and patterns of communication or the way a child thinks and understands his problems would each provide a useful but limited way to understand the child's case. An ecological model provides a way to synthesize these data to create a larger portrait of the child.

Another way of conceptualizing a comprehensive case is SNAP, or *strengths, needs, abilities,* and *preferences* (Wiger & Huntley, 2002). *Strengths* are personal characteristics or qualities such as social competence, sense of autonomy, sense of purpose, or problem-solving ability (Benard, 2004). *Needs* are defined differently than diagnoses or the presenting problems themselves; rather, they are things such as medication, after-school care, adequate nutrition, and so on that, if met, would increase the likelihood that someone will receive help from treatment (Wiger & Huntley, 2002). *Abilities* are like strengths and include skills the person has that will make it more likely he or she will benefit from a particular intervention or treatment. Lastly, *preferences* include choices and goals clients may have.

Wiger and Huntley (2002) conceptualize SNAP as a rubric embedded in the broader framework of a biopsychosocial evaluation. The biopsychosocial model is associated with the physicians George Engel and John Romano and is a way of understanding how the development, course, and cure of illness is affected by the multiple levels of an organism (Borrell-Carrió, Suchman, & Epstein, 2004). The biopsychosocial approach has many similarities to Bronfenbrenner's ecological model of human development in that both recognize the complexity of human experience. Borrell-Carrió et al. describe it thus: "The late George Engel believed that to understand and respond adequately to patients' suffering—and to give them a sense of being understood—clinicians must attend simultaneously to the biological, psychological, and social dimensions of illness" (2004, p. 576).

HOW DOES INTERVIEWING CONTRIBUTE TO COMPREHENSIVE ASSESSMENT?

Interviewing should be viewed as only one, albeit important, part of comprehensive assessment (e.g., McConaughy, 2013; Whitcomb & Merrell, 2013). The importance of interviewing can be seen in each of the perspectives discussed earlier. For example, legally we are required to assess in all areas of suspected disability and areas of unique need. As Hass and Carriere (2013) argue, it is difficult to imagine how practitioners would be able to assess in these areas without interviewing the stakeholders (e.g., parents, teachers, etc.) who initiated the referral. In addition, *IDEIA* (2004), the *R.I.O.T.* framework (Leung, 1993), and Merrell's *rule of two* (Merrell, 2008) all urge us to not be dependent on a single type or source of data. Although a child's history—as reflected in written documents, observations in a classroom or on the playground, and standardized tests of rating scales—plays an important role in assessment, interviews have the advantage of being flexible enough in their application to achieve different goals with different informants.

Interviews are also the key assessment strategy to help in building a collaborative relationship with children, parents, and teachers. In addition, it is the best approach to gathering data that will provide the insider or *emic* perspective discussed earlier. The biopsychosocial framework, which values subjective experience and the relationship between practitioners and patients, views this process of building a collaborative relationship as giving "more power to the patient in the clinical process and transform[ing] the patient's role from passive object of investigation to the subject and protagonist of the clinical act" (Borrell-Carrió et al., 2004, p. 577). This transformation is critical to both obtaining accurate information and promoting cooperation with the plans and goals that arise from an assessment. Interviews or purposeful, collaborative conversations between practitioners and the children, parents, and educators they serve are the most practical way to achieve this.

Like other approaches to gathering information, interviewing has both strengths and limitations. Also noted earlier, interviews uniquely offer the opportunity to promote a collaborative relationship with clients and to access the insider or *emic* perspective. Interviewing also offers practitioners the flexibility to respond to the answers to initial questions and follow up on important issues as they arise. Although a strength, in certain situations this flexibility also has a downside. Interviewers have biases arising from their personal histories, education, and training, which can lead them to respond to answers differently and to come to different conclusions about the issues raised by clients. When the goal is to arrive at an accurate diagnosis, then less flexibility and more structure are often required (Wiger & Huntley, 2002). But, even with increased structure, the reliability of many psychiatric diagnoses is questionable. For example, a critique of the reliability of the *DSM-5* (American Psychiatric Association, 2013) found reliability statistics of only 0.28 for major depressive disorder and only 0.20 for generalized anxiety disorder (Vanheule et al., 2014). Lastly, as discussed in Chapter 1, skillful interviewing takes considerably more training than, say, the administration of a standardized test or even using a standardized behavior rating scale. Given these potential challenges, it is important to understand interviewing as one component of a comprehensive assessment.

Chapter 2 Takeaway Points

- The ecological perspective provides a framework for understanding the systems that both cause and resolve children's difficulties. The microsystem and the mesosystem are especially important, and easily accessible via interviews with stakeholders.
- A comprehensive assessment can be understood from legal guidelines or from frameworks (e.g., R.I.O.T., rule of two, SNAP, biopsychosocial, and the like).
- Interviews are an important part of a comprehensive assessment and the only approach that facilitates the creation of a collaborative relationship and provides the insider perspective so critical to understanding the complexity of a child's difficulties and developing helpful goals, plans, and interventions.
- Interviewing is a flexible approach to assessment, but if the goal is a precise diagnosis or classification, it often lacks reliability.
- Interviewing should be viewed as an important tool but only one component of a comprehensive assessment.

References

American Psychiatric Association. (2013). *Diagnostic and statistical manual of mental disorders* (5th ed.). Washington, DC: Author.

Apter, S. J., & Conoley, J. C. (1984). *Childhood behavior disorders and emotional disturbance: An introduction to teaching troubled children.* Englewood Cliffs, NJ: Prentice-Hall.

Assistance to States for Education of Children with Disabilities Program and the Preschool Grants for Children with Disabilities Program. (2006). CFR Sec. 300.8(c)(1)(i).

Benard, B. (2004). *Resiliency: What we have learned.* San Francisco, CA: WestEd.

Borrell-Carrió, F., Suchman, A. L., & Epstein, R. M. (2004). The biopsychosocial model 25 years later: Principles, practice, and scientific inquiry. *Annals of Family Medicine, 2*(6), 576–582. doi:10.1370/afm.245

Bronfenbrenner, U. (1977). Toward an experimental ecology of human development. *American Psychologist, 32*(7), 513–531. doi:10.1037/0003-066X.32.7.513

Council for Accreditation of Counseling and Related Educational Programs (2015). *2016 CACREP standards*. Retrieved from http://www.cacrep.org/for-programs/2016-cacrep-standards/

Gutkin, T. B. (2012). Ecological psychology: Replacing the medical model paradigm for school-based psychological and psychoeducational services. *Journal of Educational and Psychological Consultation, 22*(1–2), 1–20. Retrieved from http://www.tandfonline.com/toc/hepc20/current

Hass, M., & Carriere, J. A. (2013). *Writing useful, accessible, and legally defensible psychoeducational reports*. Hoboken, NJ: Wiley.

Hass, M., & Kennedy, K. (2013). Social and emotional assessment of bilingual youth. In A. Clinton (Ed.), *Assessing bilingual children in context: An integrated approach* (pp. 163–187). Washington, DC: American Psychology Association.

Individuals with Disabilities Education Improvement Act, Pub. L. No. 108-446, 118 Stat. 2647 (2004).

Leung, B. (1993). Back to basics: Assessment is a R.I.O.T.! *NASP Communiqué, 22*(3), 1–6.

McConaughy, S. H. (2013). *Clinical interviews for children and adolescents: Assessment to intervention*. New York, NY: Guilford Press.

Merrell, K. W. (2008). *Behavioral, social, and emotional assessment of children and adolescents* (3rd ed.). London, England: Routledge.

Mills, C. W. (1959). *The sociological imagination*. New York, NY: Oxford University Press.

Salvia, J., Ysseldyke, J.E. & Bolt, S. (2007). *Assessment in special and inclusive education* (10th ed.). Boston, MA: Houghton Mifflin.

Vanheule, S., Desmet, M., Meganck, R., Inslegers, R., Willemsen, J., De Schryver, M., & Devisch, I. (2014). Reliability in psychiatric diagnosis with the *DSM*: Old wine in new barrels. *Psychotherapy and Psychosomatics, 83,* 313–314.

Whitcomb, S. A., & Merrell, K. W. (2013). *Behavioral, social, and emotional assessment of children and adolescents* (4th ed.). New York, NY: Routledge.

Wiger, D. E., & Huntley D. K. (2002). *Essentials of interviewing*. New York, NY: Wiley.

Wilmshurst, L. (2015). *Child and adolescent psychopathology: A casebook* (3rd ed.). Thousand Oaks, CA: Sage.

Ysseldyke, J., & Christenson, S. (2002). *Functional assessment of academic behavior*. Dallas, TX: Voyager Sopris Learning, Cambium Learning Group.

Ysseldyke, J. E., Burns, M., Dawson, P., Kelley, B., Morrison, D., Ortiz, S., … Telzrow, C. (2006). *School psychology: A blueprint for training and practice III*. Bethesda, MD: National Association of School Psychologists.

CHAPTER 3

Steps in Interviewing for Assessment

As discussed previously, interviews for assessment can serve different purposes. They can also have different levels of formality or structure. These approaches range from so-called nonstructured (Wiger & Huntley, 2002) to highly structured sequences of questions that typically focus on making a formal diagnosis (McConaughy, 2013). Of course, to describe an interview of assessment nonstructured is a misnomer. All interviews have an agenda or purpose and are significantly different than ordinary conversation. Another way to understand this is to think of interviews as existing on a continuum from lightly to heavily structured (Wengraf, 2001).

One way to understand the purposes of these different levels of structure is to understand the differences between *nomothetic* and *idiographic* information. When the focus of an interview is on making a formal diagnosis or classification, the purpose is to gather *nomothetic* information. That is, the information looks for commonalties that allow for deciding if a person belongs to a certain class or group. Hass and Kennedy (2013) refer to this as *membership*. When deciding about a formal diagnosis, whether *DSM-5* or IDEIA, set sequences of questions and decision rubrics (e.g., if the client answers yes to questions 1, 2, and 3, then a diagnosis of X is likely) create greater reliability or consistency between interviewers. This is especially important in medical or clinical settings where accurate diagnoses are highly valued.

When the purpose of an interview is to gather information about the uniqueness of an individual, then the focus is on gathering *idiographic* information. For example, behavioral approaches to assessment, which focus on the specific behaviors of an individual and the environment and patterns of interaction that support those behaviors, are often considered idiographic (McConaughy, 2013). When the focus of an interview is more idiographic, the goal is to gather information about the uniqueness of an individual. This requires the flexibility to pursue topics that emerge as important for someone even if they do not directly inform a diagnosis or classification.

Most situations require both nomothetic and idiographic information. For example, a diagnosis can help practitioners, parents, and educators better understand a child, but developing effective treatment recommendations will also require information about the child's unique social and cultural context and how his behaviors and symptoms manifest in that particular environment. In writing about the social and emotional assessment of bilingual and bicultural youth, Hass and Kennedy (2013) argue that comprehensive assessment reflects these two broad themes: (1) assessment of membership and (2) assessment of personal characteristics, including strengths and emotional challenges. Oftentimes personal characteristics are viewed as only individual attributes such as determination or friendliness. It is also important to consider what we might call ecological variables such as family support, community resources, or friendships. To accomplish this, a semistructured interviewing approach is often the best fit because it allows the practitioner to pursue both nomothetic information about membership and idiographic information about personal characteristics, and integrate these into a comprehensive portrait of the individual (Wiger & Huntley, 2002). In a semistructured interview, the practitioner can ask specific questions that can lead to decisions about diagnosis or classification but also has the flexibility to pursue topics that arise as important for the person being interviewed.

The way in which these different structures can result in qualitatively different information is illustrated by a study among the Navajo in the Four Corners region of the southwestern United States (Csordas, Dole, Tran, Strickland, & Storck, 2010). The authors compared the results of an open-ended ethnographic interview protocol and the Structured Clinical Interview for *DSM* (SCID-NP). They found that the more open-ended interview protocol yielded a wider picture of interviewees' lives than the SCID-NP, often revealing more than one illness or problem as well as more information about how the interviewees' social and cultural backgrounds influenced their experiences. Also, the authors found that interviewees reported more relief at being able to discuss their problems following the more open-ended interview, perhaps because the ethnographic interview allowed more opportunities for relationship-building and focused more on the unique experiences of a person rather than formal symptoms and categories (Csordas et al., 2010).

Interestingly, at the same time, interviewees were more likely to reveal sensitive information with the more structured SCID-NP. Csordas et al. (2010) argue that this might be because the more focused SCID-NP encourages a kind of objectivity or distance from a person's social and cultural context, the converse of the open-ended protocol, thus allowing interviewees to feel freer to reveal information that in another context might be judged as too private. These conclusions point to the advantages of using a flexible approach to interviewing that has structure when needed but retains the flexibility to pursue unique topics important to a particular person. The combination has the potential to generate a more complete portrait of an individual than using only one approach to interviewing would.

Steps in a Semistructured Interview

Like most social interactions, interviews have a sequence of interactions, stages, or phases (Sommers-Flanagan & Sommers-Flanagan, 2012). For example, De Jong and Berg (2013) describe five stages in solution-focused interviewing: (1) describing the problem, (2) developing well-formed goals, (3) exploring for exceptions, (4) soliciting end-of-session feedback, and (5) evaluating client progress. Shea (1998), in writing about teaching interviewing skills to psychiatric residents and other health professionals, also provides a five-step model: (1) the introduction, (2) the opening, (3) the body, (4) the closing, and (5) the termination. It is worth noting that these and similar models are found in books, like this one, where the purpose is to teach interviewing. The problem is that these structures at best only partially represent the flow of interviews in real life. Sommers-Flanagan and Sommers-Flanagan (2012) make this point when they write, "The clinical interview cannot and should not be an interaction that runs along a prescribed path from point A to point B" (p. 143). With this caution in mind, this section will also present five components to an assessment interview. These include:

1. Develop a focus by thinking through the goals and topics beforehand.
2. Open with introductions, small talk, and a yes set.
3. Make a transitional structuring statement.
4. Transition to specific interview questions or topics.
5. Close the interview.

Develop a Focus by Thinking Through the Goals and Topics Beforehand

Interviews for assessment differ from ordinary conversations in that they are more formal and the participants have distinct roles (Sattler & Hoge, 2006). One characteristic that gives interviews their formality and shapes the roles of both the interviewer and interviewee is that, whether done in a clinical or research context, they have specific purposes. In fact, they can be described as a "conversation with a purpose" (Burgess, 1984, p. 102). The steps in an effective semistructured interview begin before you talk with someone by thoughtfully considering the purposes of the interview. Although it is important to develop a focus for an assessment interview, it is also important to note that skilled interviewers are flexible. In other words, it is often the case that during the interview, information emerges that suggests another direction or goal is more important at that moment.

An initial conceptualization of these purposes can often be developed by a review of records, the *R* in Leung's (1993) acronym of R.I.O.T. A child's life in schools is typically well documented, and school-based practitioners often have access to many different types of written documentation, including grades, state and district academic test scores, teacher comments, discipline records, and so on. The extent of these records can be both helpful and overwhelming. Some of the information you might look for in these records includes:

- History of academic performance, for example, grades and test scores
- Teacher comments that describe behaviors suggestive of disorders that have a developmental feature, for example, attention-deficit/hyperactivity disorder, autism, and so on
- Medical or health problems that might account for the difficulties that led to the referral or need to be addressed simultaneously
- Significant life events that might impact functioning

These data and other information available in school records can help us develop an initial list of topics and questions that need to be pursued later in an initial interview.

Determining the purposes of an assessment interview is important because these purposes can lead to different questions and even different levels of interview structure. For example, if the purpose is to decide whether a child has attention-deficit/hyperactivity disorder (ADHD), this will shape the direction and nature of the questions of the interview differently than if the purpose is to understand the impact of being an English language learner on someone's academic progress. For better or worse, assessment interviews often have multiple purposes, making our jobs as practitioners more complicated. For example, we may work with children for whom both of the preceding purposes are salient. This book is structured around some of the common general purposes of interviewing for assessment: (a) understanding history and social context, (b) clarifying and classifying problems, (c) understanding strengths and resources, and (d) establishing next steps.

Open with Introductions, Small Talk, and a Yes Set

Often clients, whether children or parents, are nervous when meeting with a counselor or psychologists, and the first order of business is to take small steps to put them more at ease. The greeting and the first few interactions that follow serve as a transitional period between first meeting and the actual business of the assessment interview. How this is handled can go a long way toward putting clients at ease and facilitating the work that follows.

Since this book is written for school-based practitioners who most often work with children or youth, it is important to understand how the expectations children or adolescents have for adult behavior influence their comfort with adults. In one study in school, children were exposed to adults who were either reading a newspaper or playing with a toy. Children who interacted with an adult reading a newspaper reported significantly greater rapport than those who encountered an adult playing with a toy (Gurland & Grolnick, 2008). The authors of this study argue that children are more comfortable with a new adult whose behavior is predictable and consistent with their expectations for how adults behave. This suggests that, although it is important for adults to be welcoming of children and to demonstrate qualities such as warmth that will facilitate rapport, these qualities should take place within a set of behaviors that is typical of adults rather than the counselor trying to be child-like in some way, for example, play with a toy.

Sommers-Flanagan and Sommers-Flanagan (2012) suggest that practitioners follow an introductory ritual that might include (a) shaking hands, (b) offering something to drink, and (c) discussing a neutral topic as the practitioner and client move from a waiting area to a private space. My preference is to start with a simple introduction and a few moments of *small talk* before moving on to other questions. The introduction could, of course, include Sommers-Flanagan and Sommers-Flanagan's suggestions to shake hands and offer something to drink, but this will depend on many factors, including the age and cultural affiliation of the child you are speaking to. By *small talk* I mean something like what Sommers-Flanagan and Sommers-Flanagan (2012) refer to as a *neutral topic*. This can vary from commenting on an item of clothing someone is wearing that suggests an interest (e.g., sports teams, musical groups, and the like) to a brief discussion of last night's basketball game. Sometimes practitioners who have an office find it useful to furnish it with things that might be of interest to children, for example, games, toys, posters, and so on, thus facilitating small talk.

Another related strategy that could be used in combination with the preceding steps, following the introduction and small talk, is to ask a brief series of simple factual questions that help to establish a pattern of cooperation between the client and practitioner. An example of this might look like the following dialogue between a school counselor and a middle-school-aged girl:

Practitioner: ***"Hi Cynthia, my name is Mr. Smith and I am the school counselor. I don't think we have met before. Would it be okay if I asked you some simple questions?"***
Cynthia: ***"Sure, I guess so."***
Practitioner: ***"So, what grade are you in?"***
Cynthia: ***"Eighth grade."***

Practitioner: ***"Okay, did you go to school here for sixth and seventh grade?"***
Cynthia: ***"Yes."***
Practitioner: ***"How about elementary school, did you go to Central or Southside?"***
Cynthia: ***"Southside."***

Answering simple questions like this develops what has been called a *yes set* (Erickson, Rossi, & Rossi, 1976). A *yes set* is a communication strategy that involves asking a series of unremarkable questions that invoke cooperation with simple requests. The idea is that this builds up positive momentum that carries over to more complicated or difficult requests.

In addition to introductions and small talk, De Jong and Berg (2013) discuss the importance of *role clarification* as an introductory step in the interviewing process. Role clarification is an explanation of the interview process. For an adolescent, this might be:

I have some questions I would like to ask you about your life and how things are going at school. While we talk, I am going to take notes if that is okay with you. I think this will take about a half hour so you will be free before lunch.

Sometimes it is also important to explain the concerns that lead to the request for an assessment. This part of the role clarification might look like the following:

Practitioner: ***"Cynthia, did your mom talk to you about her wanting me to talk with you?"***
Cynthia: ***"No ... well, she said she wanted me to talk with a counselor about something."***
Practitioner: ***"Well, what she told me is that she is worried about you feeling really down and how that might be affecting school. She wanted us to talk to see if there was any way we could help."***
Cynthia: ***"Oh, okay."***

Make a Transitional Structuring Statement

At some point, the conversation turns to the business at hand. For this transition not to be abrupt, it is helpful to use a transitional statement that bridges the prior introductory conversation to the more focused questions of the actual interview. This transitional statement can also help to set up the structure of what is to follow. In addition, it is helpful to ask permission to begin to conduct the interview even if it is only a subtle reference such as, "If is okay with you, I would like to. . . ." This communicates respect and encourages collaboration on the part of the client by putting her in a position where they feel some control over the situation. In my more than 30 years of practice, I have never had a client say no to such a request.

To continue the conversation between the practitioner and Cynthia:

Practitioner: ***"Cynthia, did your mom talk to you about her wanting me to talk with you?"***

Cynthia: ***"No ... well, she said she wanted me to talk with a counselor about something."***

Practitioner: ***"Well, what she told me is that she is worried about you feeling really down and how that might be affecting school. She wanted us to talk to see if there was any way we could help."***

Cynthia: ***"Oh, okay."***

Practitioner: ***[structuring statement]*** ***"So, if it is okay with you, I want to start by asking you some basic questions about your classes and then we will start to talk about what is going on that might be affecting your grades. We will probably talk about what you think you are good at, what things you find difficult, and other things like your feelings about your life right now and how things are going with your friends. I know that sounds like a lot, and if you feel like it gets to be too much or I am asking too many questions, you let me know. Okay?"***

Cynthia: ***"Okay, that sounds all right."***

Transition to Specific Interview Questions or Topics

What follows the transitional statement is what Sommers-Flanagan and Sommers-Flanagan (2012) call *the body* of the interview. As I discuss earlier and in Chapter 1, assessment interviews have different purposes. These include (a) interviewing to gather background and contextual information, (b) interviewing for strengths and resources, (c) interviewing to establish next steps and goals, and (d) interviewing to establish an accurate diagnosis or classification. These specific purposes unite around the common goals of gathering information that will lead to a plan to assist a client to be more successful in school and life. At the same time, they inform the specific goals of the interview and the content of the interview questions that follow the transitional statement. The questions and strategies associated with each of the four purposes mentioned here will be discussed in more depth in the chapters that follow.

Close the Assessment Interview

To avoid being rushed, it is important to reserve time toward the end of the time allotted to conclude the interview and, if appropriate, plan for next steps. Skillfully closing the interview is an important step in building the collaborative relationship necessary for the interview process to be successful. The closing phase of the interview involves three steps: (1) compliment or affirmation, (2) summary of key points or themes, and (3) explanation of next steps.

The initial step in closing the interview is to offer a compliment or affirmation of the client (De Jong & Berg, 2013). As I note earlier, clients are often nervous when beginning an interview with a professional. In addition, interviewing for assessment often involves asking clients about things that they find distressing or difficult to talk about. Compliments can affirm what is important to the client (e.g., "From what you said, it is really important for you to pass algebra and graduate as soon as possible, so you can move on in your life") or highlight successes and strengths (e.g., "Wow, I know it has been difficult for you the last few weeks; it is amazing that you have gotten as much work done as you have").

Following a compliment, it is good practice to summarize the key points or findings from the interview (Sommers-Flanagan & Sommers-Flanagan, 2012). Following is a continuation of the interview with Cynthia:

Practitioner: ***"Thanks for taking time to talk with me, Cynthia. I appreciate that you are anxious to get back on track and graduate from high school. What you told me is that you sometimes find it really difficult to get out of bed in the morning and get to school and that you feel 'off' and not very motivated to do things with your friends or family. Does that sound fair?"***

Cynthia: ***"Yeah, I feel like I am really dragging, especially in the morning. It is like nothing is very important anymore."***

Following the summary, it is important to explain the next steps in the assessment process. This is an especially important step in reducing any anxiety the client has about the assessment. Explaining next steps can also include interim suggestions or tasks and should also include arranging for a follow-up meeting, if necessary. Returning to Cynthia:

Practitioner: ***"Okay, so we need to figure out how to get you a little more energy, right?"***

Cynthia: ***"That sounds good."***

Practitioner: ***"One thing I am thinking about is that you said you like to walk your dog in the evening. How do you feel after you do that?"***

Cynthia: ***"A little better, I guess."***

Practitioner: ***"So, what do you think about doing that a little more often, even every night if you can."***

Cynthia: ***"Okay, I can give that a try."***

Practitioner: ***"So, how about you do that and we meet again next week. In the meantime, I am going to talk with a couple of your teachers and your mom, if that is okay. At some point soon, we will have a meeting with everyone to figure out together how we can best help you get back on track. How does that sound?"***

Cynthia: ***"Okay, sounds good. Will you call me out of class like today?"***
Practitioner: ***"Sure, what classes would be best?"***
Cynthia: ***"I'm not sure ... maybe algebra or history."***
Practitioner: ***"Okay, I can't promise but I will try to make that work. So, see you in a few days."***
Cynthia: ***"Okay, see you later."***

There are several things to notice about this short exchange. Cynthia is given a task to accomplish even though the assessment process is not officially complete. This is both potentially helpful to Cynthia in relieving some of her symptoms but also provides further assessment information. If walking the dog helps, then this is useful information in developing a more complete plan. If it does not help or if she is unable to do it, this is also useful because the practitioner will know that Cynthia needs more support or scaffolding to act on her own behalf. In addition, the practitioner continues to build an atmosphere of cooperation by being transparent about the next steps in the assessment process and by continuing to ask Cynthia permission to do things in the interview and by offering her choices. These and other specific strategies for gathering information and promoting a collaborative relationship will be discussed in Chapter 4.

Chapter 3 Takeaway Points

- Most assessments require both nomothetic and idiographic information.
- A semistructured interviewing approach is often the best fit because it allows the practitioner to pursue both nomothetic information about membership and idiographic information about personal characteristics.
- The steps in a semistructured interview include (a) develop a focus by thinking through the goals and topics beforehand; (b) open with introductions, small talk, and a yes set; (c) make a transitional structuring statement; (d) transition to specific interview questions or topics; and (e) close the interview.

References

Burgess, R. G. (1984). *In the field: An introduction to field research*. London, England: Allen & Unwin.

Csordas, T. J., Dole, C., Tran, A., Strickland, M., & Storck, M. G. (2010). Ways of asking, ways of telling. *Culture Medicine and Psychiatry, 34*(1), 29–55.

De Jong, P., & Berg, I. K. (2013). *Interviewing for solutions*. Belmont, CA: Brooks/Cole, Cengage Learning.

Erickson, M. H., Rossi, E. L., & Rossi, S. I. (1976). *Hypnotic realities: The induction of clinical hypnosis and forms of indirect suggestion*. New York, NY: Irvington.

Gurland, S. T., & Grolnick, W. S. (2008). Building rapport with children: Effects of adults' expected, actual, and perceived behavior. *Journal of Social & Clinical Psychology, 27*(3), 226–253.

Hass, M., & Kennedy, K. (2013). Social and emotional assessment of bilingual youth. In A. Clinton (Ed.), *Assessing bilingual children in context: An integrated* approach (pp. 163–187). Washington, DC: American Psychology Association.

Leung, B. (1993). Back to basics: Assessment is a R.I.O.T.! *NASP Communiqué, 22*(3), 1–6.

McConaughy, S. H. (2013). *Clinical interviews for children and adolescents: Assessment to intervention*. New York, NY: Guilford Press.

Sattler, J. M., & Hoge, R. D. (2006). *Assessment of children: Behavioral, social, and clinical foundations*. San Diego, CA: J. M. Sattler.

Shea, S. C. (1998). Interviewing: The principles behind the art. In S. C. Shea (Ed.), *Psychiatric interviewing: The art of understanding* (2nd ed.). Philadelphia, PA: W.B. Saunders (pp. 3–55).

Sommers-Flanagan, J., & Sommers-Flanagan, R. (2012). *Clinical interviewing* (4th ed.). Hoboken, NJ: Wiley.

Wengraf, T. (2001). *Qualitative research interviewing: biographic narrative and semi-structured methods*. London, England; Thousand Oaks, CA: Sage.

Wiger, D. E., & Huntley D. K. (2002). *Essentials of interviewing*. New York, NY: Wiley.

CHAPTER 4

Interviewing Strategies

In addition to the basic outline or structure of an assessment interview discussed in the prior chapter, there are specific strategies that can help build a collaborative relationship and facilitate the gathering of useful information. These strategies exist on a continuum ranging from techniques designed to encourage expression with minimal influence on the direction of the interview, to more directive strategies meant to focus the client on a particular topic or move the conversation in a specific direction (Sommers-Flanagan & Sommers-Flanagan, 2012). This chapter will focus on both the communication skills needed to facilitate a collaborative relationship and more directive strategies such as questions or prompts needed to gather assessment information. Sometimes, verbal approaches to engaging a client or gathering information are limited or inappropriate. Because of this, this chapter will also focus on alternative data strategies that use art or drawing or more indirect methods to gather information.

A Stance of Not Knowing

As discussed in Chapter 1, a working relationship or alliance is important to client change. An important question, then, is, what can the practitioner do to help develop this kind of relationship? The answer to this question can be framed both as a general stance or attitude toward clients and in terms of specific skills. These skills, whether nondirective or directive, should rest on a foundation of self-awareness that allows the interviewer to suspend or *bracket* his or her presumptions about the client and his or her life.

The notion of bracketing has its philosophical roots in phenomenology (Husserl, 1931). Husserl advocated an approach to investigating phenomena that strove to set aside one's biases, assumptions, theories, or previous experiences to arrive at a direct and fresh experience of the phenomena in question (Tufford & Newman, 2012). In the context of interviewing, bracketing means to hear a client's story with fresh ears without too much interference from the interviewer's prior experiences and assumptions that spring from those experiences.

In counseling and psychotherapy, this has been described as a stance of *not knowing* (Anderson & Goolishian, 1992). Anderson and Goolishian state that the not knowing perspective is "a general attitude or stance in which the therapist's actions communicate an abundant, genuine curiosity" (p. 29). This belies a one-up stance of an expert who maybe listens but from a distance where expertise can be applied to making a professional judgment without much participation on the part of the client. Instead, the interviewer enters a conversation with a client like a curious and respectful traveler entering a foreign country.

The development of a "not knowing" stance is a long-term and continual process (De Jong & Berg, 2013). Among other things, it requires self-awareness. As Rogers and Farson (1957) put it, "a person's listening ability is limited by his ability to listen to himself" (p. 20). Self-awareness has long been regarded as important in the training of psychotherapists (Pieterse, Lee, Ritmeester, & Collins, 2013) and is often discussed in the context of interviewing for assessment (e.g., Sommers-Flanagan & Sommers-Flanagan, 2012; Wiger & Huntley, 2002). Pieterse et al. (2013) have proposed an integrated model of self-awareness training for novice interviewers that focuses on seven components: (1) personality style, (2) family of origin dynamics, (3) gender and sexual orientation, (4) racial/ethnic identity, (5) relational style, (6) social class, and (7) spiritual/religious orientation (p. 196). The goal of increasing self-awareness of the influence of these components on practitioners' thoughts, feelings, and behaviors is that interviewers will have more control over their reactions to clients and more flexibility in how they interact with them (Pieterse et al., 2013). It is beyond the scope of this book to describe all of the strategies for increasing self-awareness, but important approaches include personal therapy, mindfulness training, reflective journaling, and ongoing in-service supervision.

Skills for Developing a Collaborative Relationship

As I mentioned in Chapter 1, the skills that follow from a stance of not knowing have often been described as interviewing *microskills* (Ivey & Ivey, 2007). The microskills approach to teaching counseling skills grew out of a movement in the training of counselors that focused on the teaching of specific observable communication skills (Miville, Redway, & Hernandez, 2011). This approach, with its emphasis on specific behavioral skills, has been critiqued as being overly narrow in its focus and lacking the larger integrative framework needed to be an effective counselor (Ridley & Mollen, 2011). In part because of this, I have chosen to use

Table 4.1 Skills for Not Knowing

Less active >>> More active		
Nonverbal attending Observing Waiting	Minimal encouragers Nodding Ummm, okay, sure, yes, wow!	Echoing Paraphrasing and summarizing Complimenting Normalizing

De Jong and Berg's term *skills for not knowing* because it makes it more explicit that these specific skills do not operate in isolation but rather arise from a stance of respectful curiosity that promotes the bond and collaborative agreement on goals and tasks that are important to a working relationship with a client.

Skills for not knowing also exist on a continuum from nonverbal attending to more active strategies such as paraphrasing and accurately reflecting feelings (see Table 4.1). The following sections will elaborate on skills included in this continuum and discuss their relevance for interviewing for assessment.

Nonverbal Skills: Attending, Observing, and Waiting

Less active strategies include nonverbal attending, observing, and waiting. Carkhuff and Anthony (1979) refer to these skills as *attending* skills and argue that they encourage client involvement—a prerequisite for the later steps of self-exploration, understanding, and action. Egan refers to attending as "physical and psychological presence" (1975, p. 61). Initially, this presence is communicated nonverbally. This nonverbal behavior has been likened to the musical score in a movie in that, although we may not notice it, affects our experience significantly (Young, 2001).

Carkhuff and Anthony (1979) describe attending as *positioning*, whereas Egan (1975) uses the term *physical attending*. To provide behavioral specificity to the nonverbal behaviors of counselors, these authors break down attending into components such as facing the client; leaning toward the client; having an open, relaxed posture; and maintaining eye contact. In a nod toward the reality that these specific nonverbal behaviors might be interpreted differently by clients of different ages, genders, cultural affiliations, socioeconomic backgrounds, and a host of other factors, Ivey and Ivey (2007) describe attending as "*culturally and individually appropriate* [emphasis added] … eye contact, body language, vocal qualities and verbal tracking" (p. 15).

To arrive at *culturally and individually appropriate* attending, it is necessary for practitioners to be aware of their own behavior and of their clients' reactions at the same time. One of the advantages of interviewing is that it provides opportunities to observe clients (Hughes, 1989). Observing clients closely can help communicate the physical and psychological presence that facilitates client involvement in the process (Egan, 1975). Observing closely during an interview also allows practitioners to adjust their behavior in response to clients' reactions to their nonverbal behavior or questions. This helps practitioners be more welcoming and, as Ivey and Ivey (2007) put it earlier, more culturally and individually appropriate. When these observations are organized formally as part of the assessment process, they are referred to as a mental status examination. This will be discussed in more depth in Chapter 5.

These observations take place sometimes when the practitioner or client is actively asking and answering questions. They also take place when there is silence. I have noticed that novice interviewers, such as the students in my classes, often have difficulty with silence. To them, it seems to communicate that they have asked the wrong question or have become bogged down in some way. Their uncomfortableness leads them to try to correct their perceived mistakes by quickly asking the same question in a different way or coming up with another question to move the conversation away from the silence. David Whyte (2015) poetically captures this frightening reaction to silence in his essay:

> Real silence puts any present understanding to shame; orphans us from certainty; leads us beyond the well-known and accepted reality and confronts us with the unknown and previously unacceptable conversation about to break in upon our lives. (p. 213)

Yet, to adopt the stance of not knowing discussed previously, we must become, in Whyte's words, orphans from certainty. Given this, I prefer to use the term *waiting* instead of silence. The word *waiting* implies that we assume clients are thinking about our questions or taking a moment to gather themselves before moving on. They may be temporarily stuck in some sense but to jump in too quickly interferes with obtaining accurate information and reduces their sense of autonomy and participation in the assessment process.

In the end, although there are general guidelines to start from, being present and attentive as a listener requires considerable flexibility and self-awareness. It is also a prerequisite for other, more active strategies. In a sense, your attentiveness earns you permission to ask the difficult questions or pursue the topics that might be needed in an assessment. In the following sections of this chapter, we will discuss more active strategies, ranging from so-called minimal encouragers to active questioning and structured information-gathering activities.

Verbal Skills: Minimal Encouragers, Paraphrasing, Summarizing, and Behavioral Tracking

Minimal encouragers, paraphrasing, and summarizing are verbal skills that continue to communicate a stance of not knowing. Although more active responses on the part of the practitioner, they nonetheless fall into the category of what Sommers-Flanagan and Sommers-Flanagan (2012) call nondirective responses. Like nonverbal attending, their goal is to encourage clients to talk and facilitate a collaborative relationship.

Minimal encouragers are the small behaviors that good friends often use when listening to one another. They are verbal but, as the name suggests, minimally so. Examples include "oh," "okay," "wow," or even "hmmm." They can also include echoing clients' key words (De Jong & Berg, 2013). Hill (1978) included minimal encouragers in her categories of counselor verbal responses and defines this kind of behavior as

> a short phrase that indicates simple agreement, acknowledgement, or understanding. It encourages but does not request the client to continue talking; it does not imply approval or disapproval. It may be a repetition of key word(s) and does not include responses to questions. (p. 467)

Paraphrasing and summarizing are more active responses and require careful listening (Rogers, 1961). Summarizing involves stating back to someone what they have just said to you, including their thoughts and feelings (De Jong & Berg, 2013). It typically follows a question or a conversational prompt and the skillful use of the minimal encouragers mentioned earlier as the client responds. Paraphrasing is different in that it involves restating what someone has said using different words. Skillful paraphrasing involves distilling what the other person has said to its essence. Paraphrasing clarifies what someone has said and will often involve at least a subtle interpretation or reframing, whereas summarizing is simply a restating. Summarizing and paraphrasing both offer an occasion for the client to affirm the practitioner's understanding. Asking for confirmation of understanding can then be an opportunity to empower the client by communicating that what the client says is important. It also gives clients a chance to edit their remarks, which can lead to a fuller, more accurate picture of their experience.

For young children who often will express themselves through play or other activity, it is useful to use the strategy of *behavioral tracking* (Van Velsor, 2004). Instead of trying to respond verbally by paraphrasing or summarizing, the practitioner simply identifies what the child is doing. For example, if Kyle, age 6, is playing with Legos, the interviewer simply says, "You are playing with Legos." Sometimes behavioral tracking can include the reflection of feelings. For example, using the example of Kyle and the Legos, the practitioner might say, "Looks like you like to play with Legos" or "Seems you get frustrated when you can't put those pieces together." Behavioral tracking is a way for interviewers to verbally communicate attentiveness and presence when the verbal communication is limited.

INFORMATION GATHERING STRATEGIES: QUESTIONS AND PROMPTS

Often, when we think of interviewing, we think of questions. One of the basic distinctions among different types of interview questions is between *open* and *closed* questions. Open questions widen the conversation and encourage clients to talk more (De Jong & Berg, 2013; Sommers-Flanagan & Sommers-Flanagan, 2012). Open questions are also more likely than closed questions to encourage exploration of clients' thoughts and feelings (De Jong & Berg, 2013).

Closed questions can often be answered with a *yes* or *no* or short phrase and usually elicit specific information or facts. When adults respond to a closed question, they will sometimes voluntarily elaborate on their answers; children are more likely to respond with brief unelaborated answers (Lyon, 2014). Whereas open questions are preferred in most situations, closed questions can be useful when pursuing specific facts or information. It is also useful to establish the *yes set* discussed in Chapter 3. Closed questions should be used sparingly and are most effective when followed with an open question and paraphrasing or summarizing.

The following dialogue is between a school psychologist and Randy, a 10-year-old boy referred because he has had several office referrals for talking back to his teacher and getting out of his seat at inappropriate times. The dialogue illustrates both closed and open questions.

Practitioner: ***"Hi Randy, I am Ms. Smith, the school psychologist. I think I have seen you around on the playground. Have you seen me?" [*closed question*]***

Randy: ***"Yeah, I think I have seen you."***

Practitioner: ***"When I have seen you on the playground you were always playing soccer. Is that something you are good at?" [*closed question*]***

Randy: ***"I like soccer a lot! I play on a team on the weekends."***

Practitioner: ***"Wow! That's great. Would it be okay if I ask you some questions about what it is like for you in your class?" [*asking permission*]***

Randy: ***"Okay, I guess."***

Practitioner: ***"So, you said you like to play soccer [*paraphrasing*]. What do you like about school?" [*open question*]***

Randy: ***"I don't know … I guess I like math okay."***

Practitioner: ***"Okay, what else do you like?" [open question]***
Randy: ***"Oh, I like science. Especially when we do activities."***

Note that in this dialogue, the practitioner starts with closed questions.

With Randy, the closed questions started the conversation and developed a pattern of him answering questions. It also helped communicate that the practitioner was interested in things about Randy other than his office referrals. In a sense, they eased the way for the open questions that followed.

There are also three unique kinds of questions that come from Solution-Focused Brief Therapy (De Jong & Berg, 2013; Murphy, 2014). These include scaling questions, relationship questions, and future-focused questions. Scaling questions are self-anchored scales. Self-anchored scales are individualized scales created for individual clients and specific situations (Nugent, 2004). They are not designed to make comparisons with other persons like norm-based instruments are, but are created for an individual client to put his or her perceptions on a scale. Examples include the strategy of *subjective units of distress* in the behavioral or cognitive behavior treatment of anxiety (Creed, Reisweber, & Beck, 2011; Wolpe, 1990). Another example is the 1-to-10 pain scale often found on posters in hospitals and clinics. Scaling questions are very flexible and can be used to assess the magnitude of a problem or symptom such as depression, confidence or motivation to act, or progress toward a goal (De Jong & Berg, 2013). Scaling questions can also be useful for children who are unable or reluctant to give extensive verbal responses to questions. In the following interview, the practitioner uses scaling questions to clarify Randy's experience of math and writing.

Practitioner: ***"Randy, so, you like math and science. That's great! What subjects are the hardest for you?"***
Randy: ***"I don't know ... reading is okay but writing stuff is ... I just don't like it."***
Practitioner: ***"Okay, writing is really hard. Since you like math, can I ask you a numbers question?"***
Randy: ***"Sure."***
Practitioner: ***"So, on a scale of 1 to 10, with 1 being it is the hardest thing in the world and 10 being it is the easiest thing you can imagine, what number would you give writing?" [scaling question]***
Randy: ***"Mmm ... maybe a 4."***
Practitioner: ***"Wow, okay. Gosh, I thought you were going to say a 1 or 2. A 4, okay. How does that compare to math? What number would you give math?" [scaling question]***

Randy: ***"Math is an 8!"***
Practitioner: ***"Okay, so math is really easier than writing."***

Relationship questions widen the conversation between interviewer and client by bringing in the perspective of someone who is important in the client's life, if only through imagination. An example might be "If your English teacher was here, what would she say about how you are doing in class?" Relationship questions are especially useful for clients who are defensive or simply do not have much insight into their situations. The example of Randy follows:

Practitioner: ***"So, why do you think writing is so hard?"***
Randy: ***"I don't know."***
Practitioner: ***"Okay, sure ... okay, what if your teacher, Mrs. Lopez, was here and I said, 'Mrs. Lopez, what do you think is going on with Randy and writing?' What would she say, do you think?"*** *[***relationship question***]*
Randy: ***"Mmm ... she would maybe say I was slow."***
Practitioner: ***"Slow ... okay. Would she say she could read what you wrote but you just write it slow or ... ?"*** *[***follow-up relationship question***]*
Randy: ***"No, she can read it. I'm just slow."***

Future-focused questions are directed at how a client imagines his future and can be the first step in the development of goals. A classic example of a future-focused question in counseling or psychotherapy is the miracle question in Solution-Focused Brief Therapy (De Shazer, 1988). A short version of the miracle question is:

> Suppose that one night, while you were asleep, a miracle occurred and this problem was solved. How would you know? What would be different? (De Shazer, 1988, p. 5)

The miracle question elicits imagination and moves clients away from being overly focused on the problems and more on what they want from life (De Jong & Berg, 2013). Future-focused questions like the miracle question that lead to goals can also engender hope in clients (Pedrotti, Edwards, & Lopez, 2008). Although the miracle question can be useful in both counseling and assessment, it is only one example of a future-focused question. Other examples useful in the context of assessment include:

"If this new medication worked, how do you think things would be better?"
"If you were able to pass all of your classes, how would your life be different?"
"If this depression thing was a little better, how would your life be better?"

Continuing the dialogue between the school psychologist and Randy:

Practitioner: ***"So, Randy, if somehow we were able to help you with your writing and it worked really well, what would be different?"*** **[future-focused question]**

Randy: ***"I'm not sure ... maybe I wouldn't have to write as much or I would have more time to do it."***

Practitioner: ***"Okay, so you would have less to do and maybe more time to do what you have to do. If that happened, what would be different for you in school?"*** **[future-focused question—follow-up]**

Randy: ***"I guess I wouldn't get as frustrated."***

Practitioner: ***"And, if you were less frustrated, what would be different?"*** **[future-focused question—follow-up]**

Randy: ***"I wouldn't go to the office so much."***

In this dialogue, the practitioner discovers important information about what might be going on with Randy and what might help. For example, it seems slowness in completing written work is a problem for Randy. It remains to be determined if this is the result of fine motor difficulties, attention, or other causes. It also seems possible that Randy would benefit from classroom accommodations such as more time to finish writing assignments or opportunities to do some of his written assignments verbally. This, too, would need confirmation from other informants and perhaps other assessment methods.

Although interviewing for assessment will almost always involve both open and closed questions, too many questions can begin to feel like an interrogation, especially for children interacting with adults. Given this, it can be useful to use alternatives to questions such as conversational prompts. Conversational prompts are simple requests for the person being interviewed to provide more information. For example, it can be useful to say to a client, "Oh, tell me more about being less frustrated" or simply, "Please tell me more." Often, this can be combined with one of the skills discussed earlier, such as summarizing or paraphrasing. For example, "So, you said that with everything going on it is hard to concentrate. Tell me a little more about how those things make it hard to pay attention." Conversational prompts can function like open-ended questions, in that they elicit more expression and exploration.

Another alternative to straightforward questions is implied questions (Benjamin, 1981). Implied questions involve the practitioner thinking aloud and often make use of tentative language such as "I wonder if" or "maybe." Implied questions work best when the practitioner has adopted the stance of not knowing as discussed earlier and the "wondering aloud" comes from a place of genuine curiosity. Going back to Randy's interview:

Practitioner: ***"Gosh, I wonder what you would be like if you were less frustrated."*** **[implied question]**
Randy: ***"I don't know ... I guess I would get in less trouble."***
Practitioner: ***"Less trouble."*** **[echoing]**
Randy: ***"Yeah, I wouldn't have to go the office so much."***
Practitioner: ***"That would be cool. Can I ask you a few more questions about your writing?"*** **[asking permission]**
Randy: ***"Okay."***
Practitioner: ***"I wonder if you are slow with other things you do with your hands, like drawing.*** **[implied question]** ***Tell me about that."*** **[conversational prompt]**

Alternative Strategies for Gathering Interview Information

In addition to conversational prompts and implied questions, there are other strategies for gathering information that do not necessarily involve the straightforward asking and answering of questions. In this section I will discuss three that I have found especially useful. These include the *Typical Day Interview* (Goldston & Whiteley, 1967), *ecomaps* (Nastasi, Jayasena, Summerville, & Borja, 2011; Verlenden, 2014) and *drawings* (Handler & Habenicht, 1994).

The *Typical Day Interview* involves understanding how children and adolescents spend their time from getting up in the morning until they go to bed at night. Although the original version of the Typical Day Interview was developed as a research tool to study how students cognitively differentiated different aspects of their school day, it is also useful as an assessment tool (Goldston & Whiteley, 1967). Goldston and Whiteley recommend dividing the day into time periods: (1) time in the morning before school, (2) the school day divided by class periods or subjects, (3) time immediately after school, and (4) time in the evening before bed. In addition to the ability to differentiate the school day, the narrative responses to a Typical Day Interview can be evaluated from perceptions of teachers and subjects; use of free time; interactions with peers, teachers, and parents; ability to be independent; and presence of symptoms of mental health problems such as depression or anxiety. In the following dialogue, the school psychologist uses the Typical Day Interview to find out information about Randy's morning:

Practitioner: ***"Randy, I am curious about your day. When do you get up in the morning?"***
Randy: ***"About 7 in the morning."***
Practitioner: ***"Okay, who gets you up?"***

Randy: ***"No one. I get up by myself."***
Practitioner: ***"Oh, okay. So, what is the first thing you do after you get up?"***
Randy: ***"I get breakfast and watch TV for a while."***
Practitioner: ***"So, you make your own breakfast?"***
Randy: ***"Yeah, and then I get my clothes on and brush my teeth and go out to catch the bus."***
Practitioner: ***"Wow, you do that all on your own. Right?"***
Randy: ***"Yep."***

Ecomaps are visual representations of relationships with significant others (Nastasi, Moore, & Varjas, 2004). They have been used extensively in research in other cultures as well as settings such as family law (Hartman, 1995; Nastasi et al., 2011; Rickert & Rettig, 2006). They have the advantage of eliciting useful information about how children perceive their significant relationships from an insider's perspective. When children are asked to create an ecomap, they are first instructed to identify persons who are important to them and draw each of these persons in relationship to themselves. These visual representations can be actual drawings of persons or simple circles. Different ecomaps can be created for family, schools, peers, or friends, or a summary map can be created that represents social supports and stressors across different contexts (Nastasi et al., 2011). Once the ecomap is created, each relationship is then identified as supportive, stressful, or ambivalent, using different drawn lines (Nastasi et al., 2004). Typically, two straight lines or two lines of dots depict supportive relationships; a combination of one straight and one wavy line or one line of *X*s depicts an ambivalent relationship or one that is sometimes supportive and sometimes not, and two wavy lines or two lines of *X*s depict a relationship that is stressful or unsupportive. After children have completed the ecomap, practitioners can follow up with questions about the way they categorized their relationships that clarify why the people in their ecomaps were depicted the way they were. Figure 4.1 is a simple family ecomap that represents the relationship of a child with different members of his family.

The use of projective *drawings* in interviews of children has a long history (Terre Blanche, 2013). Although projective methods, with their roots in psychoanalytic theory, have been controversial, research suggests that the use of drawings in a "draw and tell" manner can help children provide more information about events and their emotional states (Gross & Hayne, 1998; Gross, Hayne, & Drury, 2009). For example, in one study of 5- to 12-year-old children undergoing mental health assessments, the children who drew while being interviewed provided twice as much information as those who were interviewed using only verbal strategies (Woolford, Patterson, Macleod, Hobbs, & Hayne, 2015). Researchers have speculated that drawing during an interview helps children share more information because interviewers have

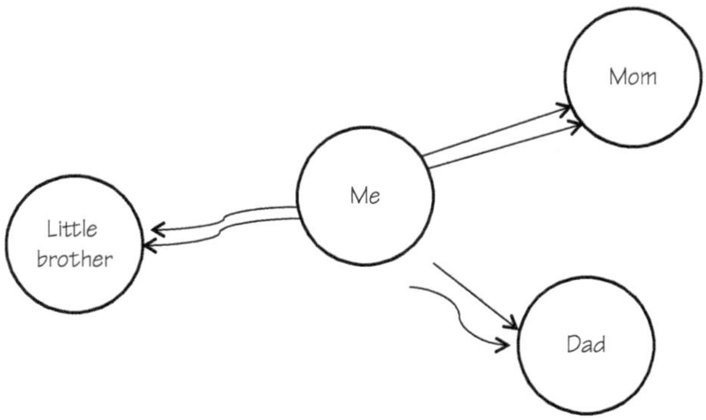

Figure 4.1 Family Ecomap

been shown to provide more supportive minimal encouragers when children are drawing than they do when the interaction is only verbal (Macleod, Gross, & Hayne, 2013).

Drawings can take many forms. Children can draw pictures of their families, their classrooms, or even their experience of a problem. This latter strategy is useful if the goal is to *externalize* the problem (Dykes & Neville, 2000; White & Epston, 1989). Externalizing the problem means that the practitioner and client engage in a conversation about the problem that assumes it is apart from the child and not part of who he or she is. For example, the practitioner may ask the client to draw a picture of the problem and then ask questions about its qualities, for example, size, shape, color, strengths, weaknesses, and so on, as if it were external to the client.

NOTE-TAKING STRATEGIES

There has been a lively debate in counseling and psychotherapy about the value of note-taking during sessions. Some studies have found note-taking to have a detrimental effect, whereas others have found note-taking did not change perceptions of therapists (Christie, Bemister, & Dobson, 2015). This has led to differing recommendations about note-taking, with some advocating for notes and others recommending that therapist not take notes. Although notes may be optional for psychotherapy, they are essential for assessment. Given this, it is important to consider how we might counteract the possible negative impact of note-taking.

One strategy is for practitioners to ask permission to take notes. Like asking permission to transition from small talk to the content of an interview, asking permission to take notes communicates respect and encourages autonomy. Also, communicating the intention of taking notes can signal that what the client says is important. If one of the goals of an interview is to build a working relationship, then our strategies for note-taking should not interfere with this goal (Wiger & Huntley, 2002). That is, the process of note-taking should not get in the way of physically attending to clients or the use of other skills for not knowing. Following is an example of how note-taking can be introduced into the interview process with Randy:

Practitioner: ***"Randy, before we get started, I wanted you to know that I would like to take notes as we talk. My memory is not great, and I want to make sure I remember the things you say. Would that be okay?"***

Randy: ***"I guess. What are you going to do with the notes?"***

Practitioner: ***"Well, when we finish the assessment, I am going to write a report that your parents and your teachers will read. We will also have a meeting where we talk everything over and come up with a plan as to the best way to help you do better in school. Some of the things you say will end up in the report. If you have any questions about what I am going to say or how I am going to talk about what you say, you let me know and we will talk it through. Okay?"***

Randy: ***[hesitantly] "Okay."***

Practitioner: ***[puts clipboard on table near Randy so he can see it] "Okay, I am going to write my notes on this notepad in the clipboard. Remember, if you have any questions, ask me ... okay? Can we start by me asking you some basic questions?"***

Randy: ***"All right ..."***

Three things took place in this excerpt. The practitioner asked permission and provided as much reassurance as possible, given the circumstances. In addition, the practitioner tried to be as transparent about the process (e.g., I will write report, have a meeting, talk with your parents). Lastly, the practitioner placed the clipboard on the table so that Randy could see it, communicating further transparency about the process.

Given that note-taking has been shown to be a cognitively demanding task (Piolat, Olive, & Kellogg, 2005), it is important to also find a way to take notes that is efficient and does not take too much away from the psychological presence needed to establish rapport. One way to reduce the distraction of taking notes is to use a format that provides at least some structure. In the same way that using a semistructured interview format allows practitioners to focus their questions on essential information yet retain some flexibility to pursue ideographic topics as they arise, a template for note-taking should remind interviewers of needed information but also give room to document other information as it arises.

These templates can be created for different purposes, depending on the goal of the interview. As I discuss in Chapter 1, assessment interviews can include (a) interviewing to understand history and context, (b) interviewing to clarify and classify problems, (c) interviewing about academic performance, (d) interviewing to understand strengths and resources, (e) interviewing in high-risk situations such as crisis or threat, and (e) interviewing to establish motivation and commitment. Templates created for each of these purposes would require different questions and topics. An example of a general template would be *SNAP* (strengths, needs, abilities, and preferences) discussed in Chapter 2 (Wiger & Huntley, 2002). A second example is the *IS PATH WARM* (ideation, substance abuse, purposelessness, anxiety, trapped, hopelessness, withdrawal, anger, recklessness, and mood changes) template for suicide assessment proposed by the American Association of Suicidology (n.d.). Other examples of templates can be seen in the appendices.

The following two chapters move away from the specifics of how to structure an interview and the basic communication skills needed to conduct an effective interview toward more advanced interviewing skills. These include conducting a Mental Status Exam and interviewing diverse clients. Following these chapters are a series of chapters discussing specific applications of interviewing. Each of these will include a case study to illustrate how these different purposes look in real life.

Chapter 4 Takeaway Points

- A stance for not knowing is an essential starting place for developing a collaborative relationship and gathering accurate and useful information.
- A variety of skills are needed to encourage disclosure and a working relationship. These include nonverbal attending, minimal encouragers, paraphrasing, summarizing, behavioral tracking, open questions, closed questions, implied questions, and conversational prompts.
- Alternatives to straightforward ask–answer strategies can often be useful. These include Typical Day Interviews, ecomaps, and drawings.
- Notetaking should be used as a way to communicate to the client and further the working relationship. Also, it is important to use interview guides or templates to take notes efficiently.

References

American Association of Suicidology. (n.d.). *Warning signs*. Retrieved May 9, 2016, from http://www.suicidology.org/resources/warning-signs

References

Anderson, H., & Goolishian, H. (1992). The client is the expert: A not-knowing approach to therapy. In S. McNamee & K. Gergen (Eds.), *Social construction and the therapeutic process* (pp. 25–39). Newbury Park, CA: Sage.

Benjamin, A. (1981). *The helping interview*. Boston, MA: Houghton Mifflin.

Carkhuff, R. R., & Anthony, W. A. (1979). *The skills of helping*. Amherst, MA: Human Development Press.

Christie, C. D., Bemister, T. B., & Dobson, K. S. (2015). Record-informing and note-taking: A continuation of the debate about their impact on client perceptions. *Canadian Psychology, 56*(1), 118–122.

Creed, T. A., Reisweber, J., & Beck, A. T. (2011). *Cognitive therapy for adolescents in school settings*. New York, NY: Guilford Press.

De Jong, P., & Berg, I. K. (2013). *Interviewing for solutions*. Belmont, CA: Brooks/Cole, Cengage Learning.

De Shazer, S. (1988). *Clues: Investigating solutions in brief therapy*. New York, NY: W.W. Norton.

Dykes, M. A., & Neville, K. E. (2000). Taming Trouble and other tales: Using externalized characters in solution-focused therapy. *Journal of Systemic Therapies, 19*, 74–81.

Egan, G. (1975). *The skilled helper: A model for systematic helping and interpersonal relating*. Monterey, CA: Brooks/Cole.

Goldston, J., & Whiteley, J. M. (1967). An exploratory study of secondary school students using the typical day interview. *The Journal of Experimental Education, 36*(2), 22–27.

Gross, J., & Hayne, H. (1998). Drawing facilitates children's verbal reports of emotionally laden events. *Journal of Experimental Psychology, Applied, 4*, 163–179.

Gross, J., Hayne, H., & Drury, T. (2009). Drawing facilitates children's reports of factual and narrative information: Implications for educational contexts. *Applied Cognitive Psychology, 23*, 953–971.

Handler, L., & Habenicht, D. (1994). The Kinetic Family Drawing technique: A review of the literature. *Journal of Personality Assessment, 62*(3), 440–464.

Hartman, A. (1995). Diagrammatic assessment of family relationships. *Families in Society, 76*(2), 111–122.

Hill, C. E. (1978). Development of a counselor verbal response category. *Journal of Counseling Psychology, 25*(5), 461–468. doi:10.1037/0022-0167.25.5.461

Hughes, J. N. (1989). The child interview. *School Psychology Review, 18*(2), 247–259.

Husserl, E. (1931). *Ideas: General introduction to pure phenomenology* (W. R. B. Gilson, Trans.). New York, NY: Humanities Press. (Original work published 1913)

Ivey, A. E., & Ivey, M. B. (2007). *Intentional interviewing and counseling: Facilitating client development in a multicultural society* (6th ed.). Pacific Grove, CA: Brooks/Cole.

Lyon, T. D. (2014). Interviewing children. *Annual Review of Law & Social Science, 10*(5), 73.

Macleod, E., Gross, J., & Hayne, H. (2013). The clinical and forensic value of information that children report while drawing. *Applied Cognitive Psychology, 27*(5), 564–573. doi:10.1146/annurev-lawsocsci-110413-030913

Miville, M. L., Redway, J. K., & Hernandez, E. (2011). Microskills, trainee competence, and therapy outcomes: Learning to work in circles. *Counseling Psychologist, 39*(6), 897–907.

Murphy, J. J. (2014). *Solution-focused counseling in schools* (2nd ed.). Alexandria, VA: American Counseling Association.

Nastasi, B. K., Jayasena, A., Summerville, M., & Borja, A. P. (2011). Facilitating long-term recovery from natural disasters: Psychosocial programming for tsunami-affected schools of Sri Lanka. *School Psychology International, 32*(5), 512–532.

Nastasi, B. K., Moore, R. B., & Varjas, K. M. (2004). School-based mental health services: Creating comprehensive and culturally specific programs. Washington, DC: American Psychological Association.

Nugent, W. R. (2004). A validity study of scores from self-anchored-type scales for measuring depression and self-esteem. *Research on Social Work Practice, 14*(3), 171–179.

Pedrotti, J. T., Edwards, L. M., & Lopez, S. J. (2008). Promoting hope: Suggestions for school counselors. *Professional School Counseling, 12*(2), 100–107.

Pieterse, A. L., Lee, M., Ritmeester, A., & Collins, N. M. (2013). Towards a model of self-awareness development for counselling and psychotherapy training. *Counselling Psychology Quarterly, 26*(2), 190–207. doi:10.1080/09515070.2013.793451

Piolat, A., Olive, T., & Kellogg, R. (2005). Cognitive effort during note taking. *Applied Cognitive Psychology, 19,* 291–312. doi:10.1002/acp.1086

Rickert, D., & Rettig, K. D. (2006). Family support ecomaps: Visual portrayals of resources for children. *Journal of Divorce & Remarriage, 46*(1–2), 85–106.

Ridley, C., & Mollen, D. (2011). Training in counseling psychology: An introduction to the major contribution. *The Counseling Psychologist, 39,* 793-799.

Rogers, C. R. (1961). *On becoming a person: A therapist's view of psychotherapy*. Boston, MA: Houghton Mifflin.

Rogers, C. R., & Farson, R. E. (1957). *Active listening.* Chicago, IL: Industrial Relations Center, University of Chicago.

Sommers-Flanagan, J., & Sommers-Flanagan, R. (2012). *Clinical interviewing* (4th ed.). Hoboken, NJ: Wiley.

Terre Blanche, S. (2013). A picture is worth a thousand words: An overview of drawing as a tool for projective assessment. *New Voices in Psychology, 9*(1), 3–15.

Tufford, L., & Newman, P. (2012). Bracketing in qualitative research. *Qualitative Social Work: Research and Practice, 11*(1), 80–96. doi:10.1177/1473325010368316

Van Velsor, P. (2004). Revisiting basic counseling skills with children. *Journal of Counseling and Development, 82*(3), 313–318 DOI: 10.1002/j.1556-6678.2004.tb00316.x

Verlenden, J. V. (2014). *Using ecomaps to assess social and emotional functioning in school-based universal screening* (Unpublished master's thesis). Thulane University, New Orleans, LA.

White, M., & Epston, E. (1989). *Narrative means to therapeutic ends*. Adelaide, Australia: Dulwich Centre Publications.

References

Whyte, D. (2015). *Consolations: The solace, nourishment and underlying meaning of everyday words*. Langley, WA: Many Rivers Press.

Wiger, D. E., & Huntley D. K. (2002). *Essentials of interviewing*. New York, NY: Wiley.

Wolpe, J. (1990). *The practice of behavior therapy* (4th ed.). Elmsford, NY: Pergamon Press.

Woolford, J., Patterson, T., Macleod, E., Hobbs, L., & Hayne, H. (2015). Drawing helps children to talk about their presenting problems during a mental health assessment. *Clinical Child Psychology and Psychiatry, 20*(1), 68–83. doi:10.1177/1359104513496261

Young, M. E. (2001). *Learning the art of helping: Building blocks and techniques*. Upper Saddle River, NJ: Merrill Prentice Hall.

CHAPTER 5

The School-Based Mental Status Exam

The Mental Status Exam (MSE) has its roots in neurological and psychiatric evaluations and is an assessment method that combines interviewing with direct observation of clients while responding to the interviewers' questions (Garcia-Barrera & Moore, 2013). It was a way for medical professionals to gather information about the mental "system" in the same way that physicians gather information during a physical by doing a review of other systems, for example, cardiovascular system, respiratory system, musculoskeletal system, and so on. The MSE was introduced into psychiatry in the United States by the Swiss psychiatrist Adolf Meyer in the early 20th century (Lamb, 2015). As explained in Meyer's *Outlines of Examinations* (1918), the MSE was an extensive set of questions and tests that allowed psychiatrists to confirm normal functioning in what Meyer called the psychobiological system (Lamb, 2015). Over time, several different protocols for the MSE have been developed, differing in length and structure (Garcia-Barrera & Moore, 2013).

The MSE process described here has been adapted for use by school practitioners as a way of systemically collecting and documenting clinical observations during an assessment (Sommers-Flanagan & Sommers-Flanagan, 2012). Although an important source of information, like interviewing in general, the observations collected through an MSE should be viewed as part of a comprehensive assessment and should not be given undue weight in the assessment process by itself.

COMPONENTS OF A SCHOOL-BASED MENTAL STATUS EXAM

The information gathered during a School-Based Mental Status Exam (SBMSE) is derived from both direct observation of the client during the assessment and from questions asked during the interview itself. This chapter will emphasize the observational aspects of a SBMSE. The components of a SBMSE include (a) appearance; (b) posture; (c) signs of health status; (d) speech; (e) activity level; (f) affect (what emotional state best describes how the student looks now); (g) mood (how does the client describe his or her emotional state over time); and (h) attitude during the interview, for example, cooperation, openness, reaction to praise, and so on.

An SBMSE includes several aspects of clients' appearance, which can provide important information about their functioning. Children's posture or how they are dressed and groomed can give the interviewer clues about energy level, emotional state, and even their ability to take care of themselves. For example, if a child is disheveled or her clothes are dirty, this might suggest that the child does not know how to care for herself or the parents are unable to provide the support needed. The stance of not knowing as discussed earlier is helpful here because it is easy to move from the observation to a premature assumption about cause. Consider the initial appearance of Alex, a 10th-grade student at a local high school:

Alex had requested to meet with the school counselor. When he entered her office, she noted that he was dressed in an old T-shirt and that his jeans were worn and a bit dirty. He was cooperative but his answers to her questions were short. He yawned frequently and his movements seemed slow. For most of the interview, Alex was slumped in his chair.

Most practitioners would consider Alex's presentation to be atypical for a 10th-grade high school student and would be concerned about his poor grooming and apparently low energy or fatigue. Yet, there are many explanations for Alex's appearance. For example, he might be depressed or he may be working long hours to help support his family or he may be using drugs and so on. In other words, although these are key observations, it is important to see them as a way of generating hypotheses that need to be ruled in or out, rather than hard indicators of a diagnosis or type of problem.

The initial appearance of a child may also provide information about his or her health status. Questions that an interviewer might ask him or herself include, *Is the child wearing glasses? Does he use a hearing aid? Does the child's height and weight seem typical for her age? Does he seem healthy?*

Think of how Amy's appearance and behavior give clues about her health status:

The school psychologist had been asked to speak with Amy because she was reported to be very inattentive and distractible in class. When Amy sat down, the psychologist said hello and reached out his hand to shake hers. She didn't make eye contact at first, and when she did it seemed to take a couple of seconds for her to figure out what he wanted. As he spoke, she looked at his face intently but quickly became distracted by objects in the room. Amy asked the school psychologist to repeat questions several times.

Again, there are several possible explanations for Amy's behavior but several observations, such as her distractibility, asking to have questions repeated, and looking at his face while he talked, suggest a hearing loss. This could easily be ruled in or out by asking Amy about it directly, looking at her records, or by having her hearing tested by the school nurse or an audiologist.

In addition to appearance, clients' speech can also provide important information. Observations about clients' speech might be as simple as if they appear talkative, make articulation errors when speaking, or use an age-appropriate vocabulary. Practitioners might also observe what speech and language therapists refer to as pragmatic language or the use of language skills in social settings (Gleason, 2005). These might include listening and turn-taking in a conversation or using the appropriate speed and speech volume for a social situation.

In addition to appearance and speech, a client's activity level can also provide useful information. Take the example of Alex discussed earlier. His movements were slow, which might indicate depression or fatigue or both. Conversely, if Alex had presented as being overly active or agitated for his age, we might wonder if he was temporarily upset about something or, more seriously, suspect attention-deficit/hyperactivity disorder or bipolar disorder or even drug use.

When conducting an SBMSE, we are interested in both emotions expressed in the moment and the client's emotional tone over time. This is described as *affect* and *mood*. Lewis, Amini, and Lannon (2000) liken affect and mood to musical notes:

Mood is a state of enhanced readiness to experience a certain emotion. Where an emotion is a single note, clearly struck, hanging for a moment in the still air, a mood is the extended nearly inaudible echo. (p. 44)

Mood, then, is a kind of increased sensitivity or tendency to experience a specific basic emotion. This sensitivity can arise because of certain kinds of experiences. For example, being yelled at or hugged before you leave for work or school will not only produce a feeling in the moment when it occurs but will also lead to an emotional tone that will persist after the event occurs. Problems such as depression, anxiety, bipolar disorder, and others can be described as the result of the brain becoming stuck on a single emotion (Lewis et al., 2000).

During the SBMSE, practitioners observe the affect expressed in the moment and gather information about how clients describe their emotional state over time. One thing to keep in mind as we discuss emotions, both as affect and as mood, is that there is considerable evidence that humans may experience a limited repertoire of emotional expression. For several decades, researchers have postulated that there were six basic emotions: happiness, surprise, fear, sadness, anger, and disgust combined with contempt (e.g., Ekman, 1992a, 1992b, 1992c; Ekman & Friesen, 1986; Ekman, Friesen, & Ellsworth, 1972). Although developmental and cultural factors certainly influence the expression of emotions, it is useful to keep in mind that clients of different ages and backgrounds will likely present with affect that falls somewhere in a limited range of choices. I have found it useful to start with a short list of basic emotional states (e.g., sad, mad, glad, scared, mixed up, and "yuck") and try to find the emotion or emotions that best fit my observations of the client.

It is also important to notice how much emotion is being expressed. This can range on a continuum, from (a) *flat affect* or the total lack of expressed emotion, to (b) *blunted affect* or a severely reduced expression of emotion, to (c) *restricted affect* or less expressed emotion than typical for a client's age and social status, to (d) *normal or typical affect* (Wiger, 2012). In addition to the amount of affect being expressed, practitioners should pay attention to the range of affect. In other words, do clients express a range of emotions appropriate for the topics being discussed, or does their affect appear to be unidimensional or constricted?

A third aspect of emotional expression to pay attention to is the congruence between the clients' affect (how they appear to be feeling to you) and mood (how they describe their emotional state). For example, if Alex had said he was feeling happy and that life was great, this would be markedly different than how he appears, giving us pause to consider why this apparent incongruence. Related to congruence of affect and mood is the match between the client's affect and the topic of discussion. For example, if our conversation with Alex was focused on failing grades in several classes, and yet he seemed nonchalant about it, this would be something to follow up on.

As previously discussed, mood is how a client describes his or her emotional state as opposed to what you infer the emotional state to be from your observations. With older children or adolescents, asking directly is often the best way to assess mood. For example, you can simply say, "So, how have you been feeling lately?" or "How do you feel about ______?" With younger children or less expressive older children, it can be useful to present them with a simple emotional vocabulary and make the assessment of mood a multiple-choice task. In keeping with the concept that there are a limited number of basic emotions, I have found *sad, mad, glad, scared,* and *mixed-up* to be a straightforward yet useful list to work with. One strategy is to visually represent the intensity or level of each discrete emotion in a chart as a bar graph or pie chart (see Figures 5.1 and 5.2). These can be set to a particular time period such as "in the past week" or "this month" if appropriate.

Assessing decision-making and judgment is accomplished by both observation and interview. One of the things we want to understand from the children and youth we work with is

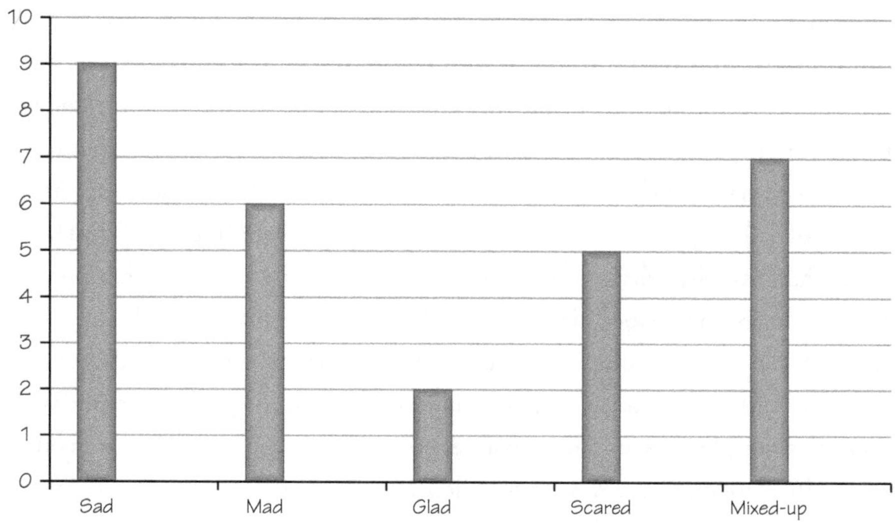

Figure 5.1 Emotions Bar Graph

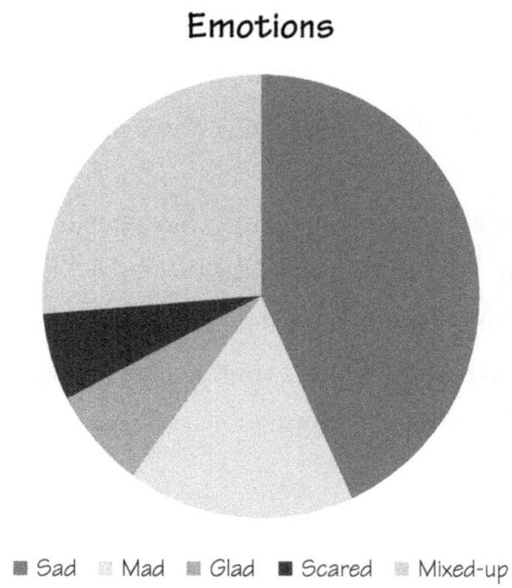

Figure 5.2 Emotions Pie Chart

how they understand their own lives. I give great importance to this insider perspective, yet at the same time, it is important to compare clients' understandings to the way their lives are viewed by others who know them well. Although children and youth will often have a different understanding of their lives than their parents or other adults, it is noteworthy when these perceptions are significantly different. Wiger proposes five levels of insight: (1) complete denial;

(2) slight awareness; (3) awareness, but blames others; (4) intellectual insight, but few changes likely; and (5) emotional insight and understanding that changes can occur (2012, p. 74).

Two examples serve to illustrate what this might look like in practice. I once worked with John, a 10th-grade boy, who was failing three of his seven classes and was on the verge of being expelled for a serious disciplinary offense. When asked how he thought his life was going on a scale of 1 to 10, with 10 being perfect, he said, "Oh, about a 9." Further questions revealed that he had little insight about his circumstances and what might happen in the future (e.g., be forced to leave the school district, not graduate from high school, etc.). This discrepancy between what was happening in his life and his perceptions led to further assessment, which revealed that he had an autism spectrum disorder that had never been diagnosed.

In the second example, I was once assigned to provide counseling to a group of middle school students in a special program for students with emotional and behavioral problems. As a way of getting to know them, I interviewed eight of them before beginning the counseling process formally. I asked each student how he or she had come to be in the special program and what their goals might be for our work together. I was surprised to find that the answers were at best vague, and most often they seemed to know little or nothing about how they had come to be there. Two boys suggested that I should call their mothers to find out. In addition, their primary goal was to get out of the program, although they had no idea how that might be accomplished.

These are, of course, dramatic examples, but they serve to illustrate the importance of understanding clients' insight into their own situation. In both cases, it was not that these youths were actively in "complete denial" as described by Wiger (2012), but they were certainly lacking sufficient insight to advocate for themselves or participate in their own treatment or educational programing. This then becomes an important component of a comprehensive assessment.

The last component of an SBMSE is the client's attitude toward the interviewer. Here interviewers can note how cooperative the client is with the assessment process. Questions that the interviewer might ask herself include, *Is the client friendly and cooperative or does he actively resist answering questions or seem guarded? How does the client react to praise or challenge?* If a client is uncooperative or overly resistant, then the quality of the information he shares can be called into question. It is important to note that often, interviewers are strangers or near strangers. Given this, a certain amount of guardedness or shyness can be typical. At the same time, given the use of the skills for not knowing discussed earlier, most children or youth will become at least a little more open and cooperative in a short time.

Documentation of the MSE

Earlier in the chapter, an MSE is described as a way of systematically collecting and documenting observations during the assessment process (Sommers-Flanagan & Sommers-Flanagan, 2012). This raises the question of how specifically interviewers can collect and document these observations. One strategy is to use an MSE protocol (see Appendix 4 for an example). Like the templates discussed in the note-taking section of Chapter 4, an MSE protocol has the advantage of reminding the interviewer of what specifically to look for or ask about. The difficulty is that it is sometimes difficult to work with two different protocols at the same time, for example, a semistructured interview protocol with content questions and an MSE protocol. Although it is possible to complete the MSE protocol soon after the interview, this compromises the accuracy of the observations because of the lack of immediacy and failures of memory.

Another strategy is to integrate the MSE observations into the interview process itself. This strategy is well suited for schools where it is unusual to conduct an MSE as a stand-alone process. One way to do this is to create two columns on paper used to take notes. On the left, I place a wider column where I record the client's answers to the specific questions I ask. On the right, I place a column where I note my observations of the client during the interview. If I want to be especially thorough, I will then use the SBMSE protocol to collect these observations and document them formally. See Table 5.1 for an example of what this might look like.

The next chapter discusses adapting interviews for diverse clients. Diversity can mean many things, but the focus of Chapter 6 will be on developmental and cultural differences. The subsequent chapters will deal directly with interviewing for different purposes, including (a) interviewing for history, (b) interviewing for diagnoses and classification, (c) interviewing for strengths and resources, and (d) interviewing for motivation and commitment.

Chapter 5 Takeaway Points

- The Mental Status Exam (MSE) has its roots in neurology and psychiatry and was developed to assess the biopsychological system.
- The information from an MSE is derived from observations of a client and from interview questions. The focus in this chapter has been on the observation aspects of an MSE.
- The data from an MSE is only one part of a comprehensive assessment.
- The components of an MSE vary among different protocols but the School-Based Mental Status Exam focuses on: (a) appearance; (b) posture; (c) signs of health status; (d) speech;

(e) activity level; (f) affect (what emotional state best describes how the student looks now); (g) mood (how does the client describe his or her emotional state over time); and (h) attitude during the interview, for example, cooperation, openness, reaction to praise, and so on.

- Documenting the observations from an MSE can be done using a protocol or template or by integrating the information into the notes from a broader semistructured interview.

Table 5.1 Mental Status Summary

Interview Questions With a Focus on Home, Health, and School Functioning	Mental Status Observations
Home/family Whom do you live with? (If there is a noncustodial parent, find out what the visitation schedule is.) Family living outside the home? **Health** Recent doctors' visits? Significant illnesses or injuries? Medication? Now or in past? Vision and hearing? **Education/school** Current school? Grade? School history, including preschool? Favorite classes or subjects? Most difficult classes or subjects? Do you get any extra help with these subjects? Who helps you? How do they help you? Recent grades? Experiences with homework? (How does the student experience homework? Is it difficult, easy, etc.? About how much homework does the student complete in a day or week? Try to get a percentage.)	Appearance Posture Signs of health status Speech Activity level Affect Mood Attitude

References

Ekman, P. (1992a). An argument for basic emotions. *Cognition and Emotion, 6,* 169–200.

Ekman, P. (1992b). Are there basic emotions? *Psychological Review, 99,* 550–553.

Ekman, P. (1992c). Facial expressions of emotions: New findings, new questions. *Psychological Science, 3*(1), 34–38.

Ekman, P., & Friesen, W. V. (1986). A new pan-cultural expression of emotion. *Motivation and Emotion, 10,* 159–168.

Ekman, P., Friesen, W. V., & Ellsworth, P. (1972). *Emotions in the human face: Guidelines for research and integration of findings.* New York, NY: Pergamon Press.

Garcia-Barrera, M. A., & Moore, W. R. (2013). History taking, clinical interviewing, and the Mental Status Examination in child assessment. In D. H. Saklofske, C. R. Reynolds, & V. L. Schwean (Eds.), *The Oxford handbook of child psychological assessment* (pp. 423–444). New York, NY: Oxford University Press.

Gleason, J. B. (2005). *The development of language* (6th ed.). Boston, MA: Pearson Education.

Lamb, S. (2015). Social skills: Adolf Meyer's revision of clinical skill for the new psychiatry of the twentieth century. *Medical History: An International Journal for the History of Medicine and Related Sciences, 59*(3), 443–464.

Lewis, T., Amini, F., & Lannon, R. (2000). *A general theory of love.* New York, NY: Random House.

Meyer, A. (1918). *Outlines of examinations*. New York, NY: Bloomingdale Hospital Press.

Sommers-Flanagan, J., & Sommers-Flanagan, R. (2012). *Clinical interviewing* (4th ed.). Hoboken, NJ: Wiley.

Wiger, D. E. (2012). *The psychotherapy documentation primer* (3rd ed.). Hoboken, NJ: Wiley.

CHAPTER 6

Interviewing Culturally Diverse Interviewees

In this chapter I will discuss diversity primarily in terms of culture or ethnicity. I recognize that this is a limited view of diversity and that there are many other aspects of persons' lives that are salient to their identities, including but not limited to national and regional affiliations, gender identity, and sexual preference, to name only a few. Although all of these facets of people's lives have important impacts on their identities, culture has a significant impact on how we communicate, how we relate to others, and how we understand and respond to problems in our lives, making it especially important for interviewing for assessment.

Even a quick glance at the demographics of schools in the United States affirms the complexity of cultural and social diversity. For example, the National Center for Educational Statistics (NCES, 2016) reports that the racial/ethnic distribution of the school-age population in the United States changed dramatically between 2000 and 2013. The percentage of school-age children who were White decreased from 62% to 53% and the percentage of children who were African American decreased from 15% to 14% during this time. In contrast, the percentage of school-age children who were Hispanic or Latino increased from 16% to 24% and the percentage of school-age children who were Asian increased from 3% to 5%. The implications of these data are simply that fewer practitioners will work in communities where most school-age children are White and English speaking, making understanding culture and its implications for education and mental health critical for assessment professionals.

Being Culturally Responsive to Clients and Their Identities

The preceding data can be deceptive in that they can lure us into thinking that these groups are monolithic or that their identities are equally influenced by their identification as Latino or African American. This easily leads to generalizations and even stereotyping. Earlier, I discussed that nomothetic information focuses on commonalties and membership (Hass & Kennedy, 2013), while idiographic information focuses on unique individual characteristics. Approaching issues of culture and social status from both vantage points is important because while nomothetic information is sometimes useful (e.g., persons who identify as Black or Mexican American are similar in certain ways, and so forth), we never interview a category but rather unique individuals who have complex identities and may or may not value the characteristics we identify with a social group. The stance of not knowing with its emphasis on what Anderson and Goolishian (1992) describe as "abundant, genuine curiosity" (p. 29) is especially useful in allowing practitioners to put themselves in a position of discovering the value clients place on certain social identities and understanding the relevance that this has for an assessment.

At the same time, some exposure to a cultural or social group is useful in that it helps us have a broad understanding of the history and worldview of a people who have a shared sense of identity. This basic knowledge along with awareness of our own identity can help practitioners not reflexively interpret someone's behavior through their own social and cultural lenses. This exposure can be accomplished through a variety of strategies, including reading literature or watching movies that depict elements of the worldview of a group, reading newspapers and periodicals that target a certain cultural group, spending time shopping, eating, or attending holiday events in communities different from your own or finding a mentor or someone who can help you by being a kind of cultural ambassador to a group (Fawcett & Evans, 2012). Although useful, it is important to remember that this general knowledge about a group of people will at best only provide a limited view of a client's world. It is even more important for practitioners to understand the uniqueness of *this* client and how she draws upon cultural and group affiliation to make her way through the world (Hass & Kennedy, 2013).

What Is Culture?

Before we can elaborate on interviewing diverse clients, it is important to have a working definition of culture. As anthropologists have discovered, the problem is that arriving at a precise definition of culture is elusive at best. One common broad definition of culture is a distinct collective pattern of behaviors that have evolved as adaptation to a unique environment (Eisenhart, 2001). This *culture as a way of life* framework assumes a distinct group of people who live in a shared but discrete environment. This approach to culture often talks about "Latino culture," "Black culture," or "Vietnamese culture." In the domains of assessment or counseling, this version of culture can lead to overly broad recommendations about groups involving eye contact or greetings, expression of emotion, and so on. It is not necessarily that these things are untrue, but rather they do not account for the nuances of identity. For example, this general perspective would not completely account for a bilingual individual born in a suburb of Los Angeles or Denver but raised in an immigrant Mexican family.

Another way to look at culture is as what the anthropologist Clifford Geertz (1973) called *webs of meaning*. Here the emphasis is more on how people make meaning of their lives through shared systems of signs and symbols as opposed to the focus on behavior and cultural practices of the "culture as way of life" approach. From this perspective, people are engaged in an ongoing process of interpreting things in the world using their shared systems of symbols. Cultural practices become significant because of the meaning people give to them, and the shared webs of meaning become a resource that people draw upon to make sense of the world.

A third way of understanding culture (there are many) is as *funds of knowledge* (Moll, Tapia, & Whitmore, 1997). Moll et al. define funds of knowledge as "the historically accumulated and culturally developed bodies of knowledge and skills essential for household or individual functioning and well-being" (1997, p. 139). The "funds of knowledge" approach to culture developed as a way for teachers to understand, value, and make use of the cultural and cognitive resources present in the households of the children they taught who came from backgrounds different than themselves (Moll, Amanti, Neff, & Gonzalez, 1992). This understanding of culture is like the culture as "webs of meaning" understanding in the sense that it views culture as a resource drawn upon to give meaning to experiences and to guide action.

The understanding of culture as a resource has a straightforward utility for interviewing for assessment. If culture is perceived as a resource, then the primary job of practitioners relative to culture becomes discovering what this mix of cultural resources is and how it works in the daily lives of the children and families we work with. There are three aspects of culture as resource that are especially important for interviewing for assessment: language, social relationships, and understandings of the problem and its solutions.

Discovering Cultural Resources: Language

For clients who come from immigrant families or homes where English is not the dominant language, the process of acquiring the practices, beliefs and values of the dominant culture begins the moment one leaves one's home culture and steps into a new cultural milieu. For some, this is the moment when they cross a border, for others the day they leave their homes to start school. This process of learning a new culture is referred to as acculturation. Although acculturation has many aspects, key is language. The maintenance of the home language and acquisition of English language skills are critical to success in school and developing new funds of knowledge.

In addition to being an important marker for acculturation, language impacts the assessment process in several other ways (Hass & Kennedy, 2013). First, knowledge of English is important in that it influences the ability of children to understand the questions practitioners ask them. This is especially important in social and emotional assessment because language around emotions and social experiences is often nuanced and heavily influenced by the network of signs and symbols discussed earlier. Given this, a first step in assessing bilingual and bicultural youth is to assess language development and usage.

Cummins (1979) conceptualized two aspects of language skills: (1) basic interpersonal communication skills (BICS) and (2) cognitive academic language proficiency (CALP). BICS emerges in social settings and is the kind of language one uses in interacting with peers on the playground or in the community (Olvera & Gomez-Cerrillo, 2011). It is often informal language that involves face-to-face interactions. CALP, on the other hand, is the more abstract language required to learn many academic subjects such as history or science. BICS is said to take about 2 years to develop but CALP can take 5 to 7 years (Collier, 1989). A thorough assessment of a bilingual/bicultural youth will require assessment of both these types of language in both English and the home language.

Although there are several standardized tests that measure language development in English, including most major tests of intelligence and many of the tests used by speech and language therapists, these tests often measure limited aspects of CALP, namely, vocabulary or semantics. This information, if available, can be filled in by interviewing the client, his parents, and his teachers. Gathering information about language via an interview can provide data about CALPS as well as BICS and general patterns of language usage.

For example, children can be interviewed directly about what language they use when communicating in specific social contexts, for example, parents, siblings, others in the household, friends in the neighborhood, adults in the neighborhood, peers at school, and adults at school, and so on. Also, children can be asked about what music they like to listen to or what language they prefer when watching television. Lastly, it is important to ask children which language they think they speak best. Much of this information about preferences and comfort in speaking a language provides useful information about BICS.

Teachers can also be asked how a student compares to others in her class with similar cultural and social backgrounds. In a similar way, parents can be asked how well a student communicates in the home language or how a certain child compares to her siblings in language development. In addition, information from clients' records can be helpful in estimating CALP, which is closely linked to academic performance and literacy. Questions such as the number of years of education in the home language, years of bilingual instruction (if available) or years of English-only instruction can be helpful in estimating where a client might be in the process of typical development of CALP in both the home language and English. In addition, because CALP is so closely linked to academic achievement, information such as grades or test scores can also be useful in assessing CALP.

The following dialogue, between a practitioner and a 10-year-old Vietnamese American boy named Phuong, demonstrates an interview focused on language usage and competence—what language young people use when communicating in specific social contexts, for example, parents, siblings, others in the household, friends in the neighborhood, adults in the neighborhood, peers at school, and adults at school, and so on:

Practitioner: ***"Hi Phuong … I am the school counselor and your teacher Miss Le asked me to talk with you a bit. She says you have been having a hard time in class lately and you haven't been getting all of your work done."***

Phuong: ***"I don't know … it's hard."***

Practitioner: ***"Oh, what's hard?"***

Phuong: ***"I don't always understand what she is teaching."***

Practitioner: ***"Okay … that sounds hard. Phuong, is it okay if I ask you some questions about speaking English and speaking Vietnamese?"***

Phuong: ***"Okay."***

Practitioner: ***"So … where were you born?"***

Phuong: ***"Here, in Los Angeles … I think."***

Practitioner: ***"How about your mom and dad?"***

Phuong: ***"Mom and Dad were born in Saigon … that's where they met before they came to America."***

Practitioner: ***"So, when you are home, what language do they speak when they talk with you?"***

Phuong: ***"Mom always speaks Vietnamese … Dad mostly speaks Vietnamese but sometimes he speaks English … he learned it at work."***

Practitioner: ***"Anybody else in your house?"***

Phuong: ***"My little sister Chi, but she is only 2 so she doesn't talk much. My mom's mom lives with us. She only speaks Vietnamese."***

Practitioner: ***"How about when you go to the store or out to eat in your neighborhood?"***

Phuong: ***"Mostly Vietnamese around our house but if we go to a big store at the mall, I speak English."***

Practitioner: ***"With your friends?"***

Phuong: ***"Some English ... mostly English I guess ... sometimes a little Vietnamese."***

Practitioner: ***"When you listen to music or watch TV, what language is it in?"***

Phuong: ***"I like English music but my mom and grandma like old Vietnamese music ... they say it is romantic but it sounds sad ... I watch English TV when I am by myself but they like to watch the Vietnamese channel."***

Practitioner: ***"Can you read or write in Vietnamese?"***

Phuong: ***"A little ... I go to this school on Saturday where they teach us how to read and write ... I am okay at it I guess."***

Practitioner: ***"Okay, last question. Which language do you think you are best at?"***

Phuong: ***"I don't know ... kinda the same I guess ... except for reading and writing ... I am better in English."***

More information is needed but this interview suggests that Phuong's usage and competence is mixed. He very well may have adequate BICS in both languages. His CALP seems mixed but is probably better in English. Despite this, it may not be adequate to understand all of the academic language used in the classroom.

Use of Interpreters

For monolingual counselors or psychologists working with children or parents who do not speak English well and are stronger in their home languages, it will be necessary to use an interpreter to conduct an assessment fairly and comprehensively. Although an interpreter is sometimes necessary, it is important to understand that introducing an additional person into the assessment process creates several complications and requires skills on the part of both the person interpreting and the person being interpreted (Hass & Kennedy, 2013).

For the person being interpreted, it is important that he or she refrain from using technical terms if possible, speak at a slower pace than typical for ordinary conversation, and be careful to speak in complete thoughts (Hass & Kennedy, 2013). I learned from the experience of being interpreted from English to Vietnamese over the course of several day-long workshops how often during a lecture I started an idea and switched gears in the middle of a sentence.

This is not a significant problem for native English speakers like my graduate students (it is something we all do), but it posed significant problems for my interpreter. I had to learn to slow down and be much more deliberate about how I presented information in English to make it easier for my interpreter.

It is also important to talk directly to the person being interviewed. During interviews or meetings, it is easy to slip into talking to the interpreter rather than the person who is answering. I have often heard some version of "ask her … " or "tell him … " When practitioners speak to an interpreter rather than the actual child or parent, they also forget to use the eye contact and other nonverbal attending skills that are important for building a collaborative relationship. Although it can feel awkward to speak directly to someone when you know he or she doesn't understand you, the practice of acting as if it were an ordinary conversation does a great deal to reduce anxiety and communicate respect.

Although families may want an English-speaking family member present when they are interviewed, it is important that this person not be the primary interpreter. This is also true for paraprofessional school staff, who are sometimes members of the same community as the family. Having a family member or community member as the interpreter can make it more difficult for both children or adult family members to respond openly and honestly when asked sensitive questions (Hass & Kennedy, 2013).

An assessment interview will also be more effective if the person doing the interpreting is prepared for his or her role (Rhodes, Ochoa, & Ortiz, 2005). This preparation can include general points such as reminders about the importance of precise translation whenever possible and informing the practitioner when a term does not make sense or does not have an exact equivalent in the language of the client. If there are interview protocols being used, it is useful to give the interpreter time to review the questions ahead of time, thus making it more likely that the language used in the questions will be interpreted in the best way possible. During a meeting, it is also important to pay close attention to seating arrangements so that the child or parent has comfortable access to the translator and the process is as unobtrusive as possible (Stansfield, 1980).

Discovering Cultural Resources: Social Supports

Culture also has a great deal to do with how people structure their network of social relationships and what they expect from these relationships. This includes what community groups such as clubs, churches, or other community organizations children and families belong to as well as how their past relationships or ancestors play a role in their identity. These social relationships are profoundly influenced by clients' sense of their cultural and social identities and are important resources in coping with the demands of life.

In the context of assessment, interviewing clients about culture and social support can take the form of straightforward interview questions regarding caring relationships, involvement in activities in the community, and access to opportunities to participate and contribute to family, school or community life, friendships and incidents of "required helpfulness," or obligations to take care of others. For example, in the following dialogue, the school psychologist gathers information from a 13-year-old Latina named Maria:

Practitioner: ***"Hi Maria, how are you today?"***

Maria: ***"Okay, thanks."***

Practitioner: ***"I don't think we have ever met. My name is Jeanne and I am the school psychologist. You may not have seen me but sometimes I talk to students when they ask me to or the teachers ask me to talk to them. Your third period teacher, Mr. Rivera, asked me to talk with you because he said you haven't looked very happy in class and I guess you are not doing all of your work.***

Maria: ***"I don't know why he said that ... I am okay ... I guess I don't get all my work done but that's no big deal."***

Practitioner: ***"Okay, before we talk about that, is it okay if I ask you some basic questions? Nothing big ... it is just that I don't know you very well."***

Maria: ***"Okay."***

Practitioner: ***'So, you are in seventh grade, right?"***

Maria: ***"Yes."***

Practitioner: ***"How do you like to spend your free time? What do you do for fun?"***

Maria: ***"Don't know ... I hang out with my friends, watch TV, stuff like that."***

Practitioner: ***"What do you and your friends like to do?"***

Maria: ***"We just talk mostly. Sometimes we go to the movies if my mom lets me."***

Practitioner: ***"You play sports or have any hobbies?"***

Maria: ***"I used to play soccer but I stopped last year. I help my mom sew stuff sometimes. I kinda like that."***

Practitioner: ***"Cool, do you belong to any clubs, teams, or go to church?***

Maria: ***"We go to church ... St. Anthony's up on 3rd Street."***

Practitioner: ***"Oh, okay ... what is that like for you?"***

Maria: ***"Okay, I like Father Serrano ... he teaches the youth group. He is pretty nice."***

Practitioner: ***"Maria, can I ask you something about your family?"***

Maria: ***"Sure."***

Practitioner: ***"So who are you closest to in your family?***

Maria: ***"My mom and my Tia Maria ... I was named after her."***

Practitioner: ***"Oh wow, do you see her often?"***

Maria: ***"Yeah ... she lives nearby and sometimes takes me shopping and stuff."***
Practitioner: ***"That's great ... so, can I switch gears and ask you a few questions about Mr. Rivera's class?"***
Maria: ***"All right."***

The school psychologist in this example has learned several things about Maria's social network and how these resources play out in her life. There is more to learn regarding the problem, but these questions provide a useful sociocultural backdrop to Maria's life and the current problem.

In addition to current social resources, clients draw upon a past network of social relationships that can be important to their sense of identity. These networks can also extend across time in that some cultures regard relationships with long dead ancestors or cultural icons as equally important to relationships with living people. For the purposes of assessment, this suggests that behind a behavior are not only thoughts and feelings but also a kind of internal dialogue with messages clients have received from what Pedersen, Crethar, and Carlson (2008) call "cultural teachers."

In the following dialogue, Cong's teacher has referred him to the school counselor because he seems lethargic and withdrawn. In this scenario, the practitioner and Cong began the interview by discussing language and how people not alive in the ordinary sense continue to guide and sometimes inspire him:

Practitioner: ***"Hi Cong, I am Mr. Hart, the school counselor. I was in your class the other day and I remember seeing you. Did you see me?"*** ***[*****closed question*****]***
Cong: ***"Okay, yeah ... I think so."***
Practitioner: ***"I know the name Cong can be Chinese or Vietnamese. Tell me about your family."*** ***[*****open question*****]***
Cong: ***"We're Vietnamese. My dad was born in Hue and my mom is from Saigon. They met here, though."***
Practitioner: ***"Oh, okay. So, when you speak with them at home, what language do you speak, English or Vietnamese?"***
Cong: ***"Both Vietnamese and English sometimes with my dad, but mostly Vietnamese with my mom ... I have a grandma at home too. She only speaks Vietnamese. She is from Hue and she is really hard to understand for me."***
Practitioner: ***"Anybody else live in your house?"***
Cong: ***"Yeah ... my older sister."***
Practitioners: ***"What do you speak with her?"***
Cong: ***"Mostly English ... sometimes Vietnamese but she is always correcting me."***

Practitioner: ***"Oh, I guess big sisters can be bossy sometimes."***

Cong: ***"Yeah!"***

Practitioner: ***"You said you live with your grandmother. You said she was from Hue so I guess that is your dad's mom."***

Cong: ***"Yeah."***

Practitioner: ***"So, what about your grandfather?"***

Cong: ***"He died a long time ago ... he was a teacher in Vietnam and my grandmother and dad say he was really smart. They named me after him ... the name Cong means smart I guess."***

Practitioner: ***"Oh ... okay. So, they think you are pretty smart then."***

Cong: ***"Not sure ... I guess so ... sometimes they tell me to light incense and say prayers to him when I am studying."***

Practitioner: ***"How does that work do you think?"***

Cong: ***"I am not sure ... sometimes I think it helps."***

Practitioner: ***"Wow, well that's good, right?"***

Cong: ***"Yeah ... it seems strange but yeah, I think so. It feels good to know he is there in a way."***

Although the school counselor has not yet begun to gather information directly about Cong's withdrawal, the recognition of Cong's grandfather as an important "cultural teacher" and resource for him provides important information about Cong and what resources he can draw upon to cope with whatever challenge he is facing.

DISCOVERING CULTURAL RESOURCES: UNDERSTANDING CULTURAL INFLUENCES ON CLIENTS' VIEW OF PROBLEMS AND THEIR SOLUTIONS

In addition to language and social networks, culture also influences what we perceive as a problem, how we describe that problem, and how we understand its solutions. Understanding this is critical for the assessment process. This is true not only for those who identify with a so-called minority culture or for clients who simply differ culturally from the interviewer, but for everyone. Yet, it is especially important for us to carefully attend to these issues when it appears that someone's understanding of a problem is significantly different from how we might understand the problem.

The *DSM-5* (American Psychiatric Association [APA], 2013) contains guidelines for questions that help clarify the contribution of culture to diagnosis and treatment (DeSilva, Aggarwal, & Lewis-Fernandez, 2015). The *Cultural Formulation Interview* (CFI) grew out of work done by psychiatrists and medical anthropologists that dates to the *DSM-IV* (APA, 1994). It consists of four parts:

1. Cultural definition of the problem
2. Cultural perceptions of the cause, context, and support
3. Cultural factors that affect self-coping and past help-seeking
4. Cultural factors that affect current help-seeking

The CFI core module has 16 open-ended questions designed to gather information about each of the preceding four topics. Although the CFI was developed to provide a better understanding of how culture influences clients' perceptions of their problems and how those problems might be resolved, it is important to note that these topics and questions are useful because culture is, of course, present in the lives of all of the children and families we work with. In this section I will focus on the first domain of the CFI.

Questions related to obtaining a cultural definition of the problem have three goals. One is to obtain a personal narrative or story about the problem. As I discuss in Chapter 1, the insider or *emic* perspective is critical for assessment in that it provides ecological validity for other data. It is especially important when working with children or families who are likely to have a different understanding of the problem than the one informed by our professional framework (itself culturally derived). The stance of *not knowing* asks that we put aside our professional knowledge of problems and their solutions, at least temporarily, to allow for our clients to explain how they see the problem.

Asking for a personal narrative is common practice in interviewing for assessment. The CFI takes this a step further and asks clients how they describe the situation to those closest to them. This expands the description of the problem and allows for more cultural nuance than how children or family members describe the problem to a professional. In addition to asking clients how they describe the problem to others, it is, of course, helpful to ask parents or other caregivers directly.

In addition to asking important adults directly, it can also be useful to ask *relationship questions* (De Jong & Berg, 2013). Relationship questions allow the interviewer to access how the client perceives the understanding of others. For example, during an interview, a practitioner might ask a client, "If your mom was here, what would she say about this?" Thinking of the earlier dialogue with Cong, a relationship question might be "What would your grandfather say about how things are going for you now and what you need to do to make it better?"

The third goal of this part of the CFI is to figure out what about the problem is most troubling. Another way of understanding this is that the interviewer is interested in what it is about the "problem" that makes it a problem (De Jong & Berg, 2013). This can consist of simple questions such as "What about this bothers you the most?" or "So, you are failing math. What about that is a problem for you?" Asking what about the problem is most difficult or troubling helps us understand impairment or how the problem affects someone in day-to-day life. It also provides useful information about possible goals for later intervention (DeSilva et al., 2015).

The following dialogue between 16-year-old Tomás and the school psychologist demonstrates how these questions might unfold in an interview. Tomás is not going to school consistently after a period when he had attended regularly and done well. For the sake of brevity, I have skipped some of the dialogue that might have preceded this part of the interview.

Practitioner: ***"Tomás, I am interested in how you see things. You were going to school for a while, doing pretty good, and now you have almost stopped coming. What is going on from your perspective?"*** *[***asking for a personal narrative***]*

Tomás: ***"I don't know … I started going to work with my dad … he's got a business. He makes pretty good money and says it is better if I help."***

Practitioner: ***"Oh, what kind of business does he have?"***

Tomás: ***"He works as a roofer."***

Practitioner: ***"So, he owns the business?"***

Tomás: ***"Not really, but he is the foreman."***

Practitioner: ***"Good for him … that's cool. I bet roofing is hard work."***

Tomás: ***"Geez … you bet … it is really hard carrying that stuff up and down ladders all day. I am getting really strong."***

Practitioner: ***"Oh, how about school? What do you think about that?"*** *[***more inquiry about personal narrative***]*

Tomás: ***"I don't know … I want to go to school. I miss my friends and I want to go to college someday. My dad says he wants me to go too but I think he needs my help."***

Practitioner: ***"What do you say to your mom or dad or other people about not going to school?"*** *[***How problem is described to those closest to him***]*

Tomás: ***"I say I am taking some time off but I will go back."***

Practitioner: ***"And what if your dad was here, what would he say if I asked him about school?"*** *[***relationship question to gather more detail***]*

Tomás: ***"He would say that he doesn't really want me to work so hard when I grow up … like I should go to school and do something else."***

Practitioner: ***"Okay ... so what is the worst part of not going to school, for you?" [worst part of problem]***
Tomás: ***"Not seeing my friends."***

The questions asked by the practitioner in this dialogue allow for the social and cultural elements of the situation to be unpacked. At the same time, it is also clear that these questions would have utility with many different clients. No matter the cultural or social context or whether you are conducting a formal or informal assessment, understanding the client's perspective on the problem with all of its cultural and social influences is critical to successful interviewing for assessment.

In the next chapter, we examine strategies for interviewing clients of different ages. The principle of using both a nomothetic and idiographic perspective is applied again to understanding children at different stages of development.

Chapter 6 Takeaway Points

- Changing demographics in the United States make understanding culture and its implications for education and mental health critical for assessment professionals.
- Although knowledge of group characteristics can be useful, it can also lead to stereotyping. Both a nomothetic and idiographic perspective are needed.
- A precise definition of culture is elusive but viewing culture as a resource drawn upon to give meaning to experiences and to guide action is useful for practitioners conducting assessments.
- There are three aspects of culture as resource that are especially important for interviewing for assessment: language, social relationships, and understanding of the problem and its solutions.
- Language skills can be conceptualized as having two components: basic interpersonal communication skills (BICS) and cognitive academic language proficiency (CALP).
- Using an interpreter requires specific skills on the part of the speaker and interpreter.
- Culture plays an important role in how people structure their network of social relationships and what they expect from these relationships. This includes what community groups such as clubs, churches, or other community organizations children and families belong to as well as how their past relationships or ancestors play a role in their identity.
- Culture influences what we perceive as a problem, how we describe that problem and how we understand its solutions. Questions drawn from the Cultural Formulation Interview (CFI) provide a useful framework for gathering this information.

References

American Psychiatric Association. (1994). *Diagnostic and statistical manual of mental disorders* (4th ed.). Washington, DC: Author.

American Psychiatric Association. (2013). *Diagnostic and statistical manual of mental disorders* (5th ed.). Washington, DC: Author.

Anderson, H., & Goolishian, H. (1992). The client is the expert: A not-knowing approach to therapy. In S. McNamee & K. Gergen (Eds.), *Social construction and the therapeutic process* (pp. 25–39). Newbury Park, CA: Sage.

Collier, V. (1989). How long? A synthesis of research on academic achievement in a second language. *TESOL Quarterly, 21,* 509–531.

Cummins, J. (1979). Linguistic interdependence and the educational development of bilingual children. *Review of Educational Research, 49,* 222–251.

De Jong, P., & Berg, I. K. (2013). *Interviewing for solutions*. Belmont, CA: Brooks/Cole, Cengage Learning.

DeSilva, R., Aggarwal, N. K., & Lewis-Fernandez, R. (2015, June 30). The *DSM-5* Cultural Formulation Interview and the evolution of cultural assessment in psychiatry. *Psychiatric Times*.

Eisenhart, M. (2001). Educational ethnography past, present, and future: Ideas to think with. *Educational Researcher, 30*(8), 16–27.

Fawcett, M. L., & Evans, K. M. (2012). *Experiential Approach for Developing Multicultural Counseling Competence*. Thousand Oaks, CA: Sage.

Geertz, C. (1973). *The interpretation of cultures: Selected essays by Clifford Geertz*. New York, NY: Basic Books.

Hass, M., & Kennedy, K. (2013). Social and emotional assessment of bilingual youth. In A. Clinton (Ed.), *Assessing bilingual children in context: An integrated* approach (pp. 163–187). Washington, DC: American Psychology Association.

Moll, L. C., Amanti, C., Neff, D., & Gonzalez, N. (1992). Funds of knowledge for teaching: Using a qualitative approach to connect homes and classrooms. *Theory into Practice, 31*(2), 132–141.

Moll, L. C., Tapia, J., & Whitmore, K. F. (1997). Living knowledge: The social distribution of cultural resources for thinking. In G. Salomon (Ed.), *Distributed cognitions: Psychological and educational considerations* (pp. 139–163). New York, NY: Cambridge University Press.

National Center for Educational Statistics. (2016, May). *The condition of education 2016*. Retrieved from http://nces.ed.gov/programs/coe/indicator_cge.asp

Olvera, P., & Gomez-Cerrillo, L. (2011). A bilingual (English and Spanish) psychoeducational assessment MODEL grounded in Cattell-Horn Carroll (CHC) theory: A cross battery approach. *Contemporary School Psychology, 15,* 117–127.

References

Rhodes, R., Ochoa, S. H., & Ortiz, S. (2005). *Assessing culturally and linguistically diverse students*. New York, NY: Guilford Press.

Pedersen, P. B., Crethar, H. C., & Carlson, J. (2008). Conclusion: Developing multicultural awareness, knowledge, and skill. In *Inclusive cultural empathy: Making relationships central in counseling and psychotherapy* (pp. 223–241). Washington, DC: American Psychological Association. doi:10.1037/11707-011

Stansfield, M. (1980). Psychological issues in mental health interpreting. In F. Caccamise, J. Standgarone, & M. Mitchell-Caccamise (Eds.), *A century of deaf awareness* (pp. 102–114). Silver Spring, MD: Registry of Interpreters for the Deaf.

CHAPTER 7

Strategies for Interviewing Young Children

It is a given that interviewing a 7-year-old child is different than interviewing a 17-year-old adolescent and that skillful interviewing requires practitioners to be sensitive to these differences. The purpose of this chapter is to unpack some of these differences and to provide guidelines for how practitioners might apply knowledge of child and adolescent development to interviewing for assessment. To achieve these goals, it is important to understand the significant ways that children are the same and different as they develop. It is also important to understand that many of the ways we describe children of different ages are generalizations and that there are considerable differences among children of the same age (Holmbeck, Greenley, & Franks, 2003). Knowledge of the broad patterns of child development is important but does not necessarily tell us all that we need to know to effectively interview a certain child. Developmental sensitivity requires that we match the demands of the interview to the capacity of the child, regardless of the expected developmental outcomes associated with that child's age. This involves understanding the implications of emotional, cognitive, and language and development for interviewing for assessment.

Emotions

As discussed in Chapter 5, there is a body of research based on analyses of facial expressions that proposes that there are only six basic emotions, including anger, disgust, fear, happiness, sadness, and surprise (Ekman, 1972). We know that even young infants, long before they can walk or talk, are fascinated with facial expressions and can distinguish these emotions on the faces of others (Lewis, Amini, & Lannon, 2000). This suggests that emotional development is intimately tied to a child's relationship to others and that the capacity to express and recognize emotions evolved as a system of communication that allowed humans to detect the inner states of others. This then facilitated essential interpersonal life tasks (Ekman, 1992a, 1992b, 1992c, 2003; Lewis, Amini, & Lannon, 2000).

This model of a limited set of basic emotions suggests that the emotions experienced by children, even young children, may not be as different from adolescents or adults as it might seem. Given this, it is important to keep in mind that children of different ages will present with the same basic set of emotional experiences. At the same time, it seems obvious that adolescents often express their emotions using much more nuanced language than younger children can. It is also clear that emotional self-regulation changes with development. For example, a toddler may express strong emotions in a social situation that seems inappropriate to an adult, such as a supermarket or restaurant, whereas a typical 10-year-old will have developed more restraint. These apparent differences seem to be more a function of increased capacity for self-expression, self-control, self-awareness, and awareness of others.

Cognition and Language

Among the most important models of cognitive development is that of Jean Piaget (Piaget, 2001; Piaget & Inhelder, 2000). Per Piagetian theory, children's thinking develops from less to more logical and abstract thought. This progression is conceptualized as occurring in stages. The stages that encompass school-age children include (a) the preoperational stage (2 to 7 years); (b) concrete operations (7 to 11 years); and (c) formal operations (11 years and up).

Children in the *preoperational stage* (2 to 7 years) begin to develop the ability to represent objects symbolically with words. This facilitates pretend play because to pretend that a block is a car, the child must first possess a mental representation or symbol of a car and understand the difference between pretend objects and real objects. The development of pretend play facilitates further cognitive development as well as social competence (Lutz & Sternberg, 1999).

Despite the emergence of this ability to use symbols (language) to represent a concrete object, children at this age tend to remain concrete in their thinking. It is difficult for them to focus on more than one attribute or aspect of an object or situation, and they have difficulty understanding the viewpoint of other people (McConaughy, 2013). Children from 2 to 7 years old develop vocabulary rapidly and can describe both present and past experiences, although their use of past tense and even a sense of time is not well developed.

They will also have a limited vocabulary to describe emotions and will often need concrete referents such as puppets, art materials, or toys to help them to describe events or their own inner states.

During the stage of *concrete operations* (age 7 to 11), children begin to develop the ability to manipulate their symbolic representations of objects internally (Piaget, 1989). Their thinking becomes more logical and adult-like, but their application of these mental operations is still limited to concrete objects at hand. They can think logically about a concrete object but are less able to think logically about abstract symbols (Lutz & Sternberg, 1999). Children of this age are less egocentric and have more sophisticated language but still benefit from concrete aids to help them describe or think about things.

As children enter Piaget's state of *formal operations* (11 years and up), they are better able to understand cause and effect, to think abstractly, and to consider things that are hypothetical or abstract (Piaget, 2001; Piaget & Inhelder, 2000). Abstract thinking allows older children to go beyond concrete properties of the objects at hand and to think logically about symbols. As children enter adolescence, they learn to use cognitive tools such as deductive reasoning and systematic planning to carry out tasks. Their language becomes adult-like, and they can entertain hypothetical situations and play with language by using humor such as puns or riddles (Piaget, 1976).

Another difference between younger and older children not discussed in depth by Piaget is memory. Older children and adolescents make use of self-questioning and other metacognitive strategies to help remember information (Saywitz & Snyder, 1996). Younger children are more dependent on adult scaffolding in the form of adult questions or prompts to be systematic in how they recall information.

Strategies

As discussed earlier, evidence suggests that children have greater rapport with adults who have typical adult behavior (Gurland & Grolnick, 2008). This is important to consider because it suggests that children are more comfortable with adults who are predictable rather than those who change their behavior to be more child friendly. This is not to say that the use of toys, art materials, or puppets is not useful but it is important to remember that these childlike materials should be used in the context of an adult–child relationship.

In working with younger children, it is important to use shorter sentences and avoid complex grammar such as passive voice or subjunctive tenses, that is, sentences that lack a subject or do not describe concrete objects (Saywitz & Camparo, 1998). Also, research on interviewing child witnesses in forensic psychology strongly suggests interviewers avoid using questions that can be answered yes or no (Cederborg, Orbach, & Sternberg, 2000;

Steward, Bussey, Goodman, & Saywitz, 1993) and that open-ended questions or conversational prompts yield more accurate and detailed responses than more directive questions (Cederborg et al., 2000).

Following is a dialogue between a school psychologist and Tina, a 5-year-old kindergarten student who was referred because she cries each day when dropped off. This has been going on long past the time when other children in her class have settled in and are less anxious. The dialogue illustrates questions and strategies that work and do not work well for Tina's level of development.

Practitioner: ***"Hi, Tina."***

Tina: ***[nods but doesn't say anything]***

Practitioner: ***"So Tina, do you know why we are talking?"*** ***[*****This is a yes-no question that has the expectation of elaboration. In addition, given that children, even young children, know that adults know the answer, it puts a great deal of pressure on young children to get it right*****]***

Tina: ***"No."***

Practitioner: ***"Okay, let me try to explain. I heard you were crying a lot when your mom drops you off."*** ***[*****This is not a question. Rather, it is a statement that implies the child will respond with more detail*****]***

Tina: ***[no response; looks away]***

Practitioner: ***"Okay, Tina, do you like to draw?"*** ***[*****Practitioner switches tactics*****]***

Tina: ***[nods]***

Practitioner: ***"Okay, let's draw a picture of school. I will start and then you finish, okay?"*** ***[*****starting the drawing provides scaffolding*****]***

Tina: ***"Okay."***

Practitioner: ***[takes a piece of paper and draws an outline of a building that looks like the school] "I started so I want you to add the people, okay?"***

Tina: ***"Okay." [begins to draw three simple people at different places on the paper]***

Practitioner: ***[after a few minutes] "Wow! That is great, Tina ... please tell me who those people are."***

Tina: ***"My teacher ... my mom ... and my friend."***

Practitioner: ***"Great, thanks, Tina ... tell me about school ... as much as you can."***

Tina: ***[begins to talk about the building and people she drew]***

In this interview, the practitioner started by asking questions that were difficult for Tina to answer because the language was sophisticated for a 5-year-old. The practitioner then switched strategies and began to help Tina by creating a drawing to provide some concrete scaffolding for their conversation about school. The conversation ended with the practitioner using an open-ended prompt for Tina to begin talking about school.

In discussing interviewing child witnesses, Lyon (2014) proposes that prior to asking a child about sensitive material, the interviewer offer a simple set of interview instructions and ask nonthreatening questions that allow the child to practice answering interview questions. Saywitz and Snyder (1996) have also suggested that it is useful to use reminder cards as visual cues for different parts of the conversation. The drawing created by Tina during the earlier dialogue served a similar purpose. As part of these interview instructions, the practitioner could also teach a basic set of emotional terms—in this case, reminder cards with faces matching each of the six basic emotions (i.e., anger, disgust, fear, happiness, sadness, and surprise). An adaption of Lyon's (2014) instructions for school-based practitioners could include:

1. "I am going to ask you a lot questions. It's okay to say, 'I don't know.'"
2. "It's also okay to tell me you don't understand something I ask."
3. "We are going to talk about feelings so I want to teach you some words you can use to tell me how you feel. The words we are going to use are sad, mad, glad, scared, surprised, yuck, and mixed-up. Let's go though of those one by one."

Role-play practice can follow this set of instructions. Next, a different practitioner interviews 6-year-old Christopher. Christopher was referred because his teacher thinks he is starting to become aggressive with the other students in his class.

Practitioner: ***"Hi Christopher ... I am going to ask you some questions about school but before I do that, I want to play a game where we practice. Would that be okay?"***

Christopher: ***[nods but doesn't say anything]***

Practitioner: ***"Okay, ready?"***

Christopher: ***[nods again]***

Practitioner: ***"Before we start, I wanted to let you know that if I ask you something you don't know, it is okay to say, 'I don't know.' Let's try that out ... How big is the moon?"***

Christopher: ***[smiles] "I don't know!"***

Practitioner: ***"That's great, thanks ... okay, second thing. Sometimes, I might ask you a question about how you feel. To make it easy, we are going to use these feelings ... sad, glad, mad, scared, and yuck ... we can add mixed-up in case you aren't sure. So, I have these cards here and each one has a face on it. Can you tell me the feeling that goes with this card?"***

Christopher: ***"Mad."***

Practitioner: ***"Okay, and this one?"***

Christopher: ***"Yuck!" [smiles]***

[They continue, completing all the cards.]

Practitioner: ***"Okay, now let's practice some questions … What is your name?"***

Christopher: ***"Christopher."***

Practitioner: ***"How old are you?"***

Christopher: ***"Six."***

Practitioner: ***"Last practice one … what grade are you in?"***

Christopher: ***"First grade."***

Practitioner: ***"Okay, now, I am going to ask you some questions about school … I will say something about school and you point to the card that goes best with that thing, okay?"***

Christopher: ***"Okay."***

Practitioner: ***"Great … recess."***

Christopher: ***"That one." [glad]***

Practitioner: ***"Okay, so you can pick more than one if you want. Is there another one that goes with recess?"***

Christopher: ***"I don't know … mad." [points to card]***

Practitioner: ***"So glad and mad … okay, can you tell me a recess story that goes with glad?"***

The practitioner continues eliciting both feelings and stories about those feelings for recess and later classroom activities. The preparatory instructions, simple practice (like the yes set described in Chapter 3), and the visual cues provided by the feeling cards are all examples of how to provide the additional scaffolding and concreteness needed to assist young children to engage meaningfully in an interview and—most importantly for interviewing for assessment—to provide more accurate and complete information about their lives. The next chapter focuses on interviewing to clarify problems as well as interviewing to determine a diagnosis or classification.

Chapter 7 Takeaway Points

- Although children at the same point in development have many similarities, they continue to have significant differences.
- It is likely that there are only a limited number of basic emotions, including anger, disgust, fear, happiness, sadness, and surprise. These appear to be present early in life and do not vary with development.

- Although these basic emotions do not vary with development, the expression of emotions differs with the development of language and emotional self-control.
- Cognitive development progresses from more to less concrete. Abstract thinking emerges as children learn to manipulate symbols rather than concrete objects themselves.
- Memory becomes more independent of external cues as children develop. Older children make use of metacognitive strategies to assist their memories, whereas younger children are more dependent on adult cues and questions.
- In working with younger children, it is important to use shorter sentences and avoid complex grammar such as passive voice or subjunctive tenses, that is, sentences that lack a subject or do not describe concrete objects.
- Open-ended questions or conversational prompts yield more accurate and detailed responses than more directive questions.
- Interview instructions and the opportunity to practice being interviewed also improve accuracy and detail.

References

Cederborg, A., Orbach, Y., & Sternberg, K. J. (2000). Investigative interviews of child witnesses in Sweden. *Child Abuse & Neglect, 24*(10), 1355–1361.

Ekman, P. (1972). Cross-cultural studies of facial expression. In P. Ekman (Ed.), *Darwin and facial expression: A century of research in review* (pp. 169–222). New York, NY: Academic Press.

Ekman, P. (1992a). An argument for basic emotions. *Cognition and Emotion, 6*, 169–200.

Ekman, P. (1992b). Are there basic emotions? *Psychological Review, 99*, 550–553.

Ekman, P. (1992c). Facial expressions of emotions: New findings, new questions. *Psychological Science, 3*(1), 34–38.

Ekman, P. (2003). *Emotions revealed: Recognizing faces and feelings to improve communication and emotional life*. New York, NY: Times Books/Henry Holt.

Gurland, S. T., & Grolnick, W. S. (2008). Building rapport with children: Effects of adults' expected, actual, and perceived behavior. *Journal of Social & Clinical Psychology, 27*(3), 226–253.

Holmbeck, G. N., Greenley, R. N., & Franks, E. A. (2003). Developmental issues and considerations in research and practice. In A. E. Kazdin & J. R. Weisz (Eds.), *Evidence-based psychotherapies for children and adolescents* (pp. 21–40). New York, NY: Guilford Press.

Lewis, T., Amini, F., & Lannon, R. (2000). *A general theory of love*. New York, NY: Random House.

Lutz, D. J., & Sternberg, R. J. (1999). Cognitive development. In M. H. Bornstein & M. E. Lamb (Eds.), *Developmental psychology: An advanced textbook* (4th ed., pp. 275–311). Mahwah, NJ: Erlbaum.

Lyon, T. D. (2014). Interviewing children. *Annual Review of Law & Social Science, 10*(5), 73–89.

McConaughy, S. H. (2013). *Clinical interviews for children and adolescents: Assessment to intervention*. New York, NY: Guilford Press.

Piaget, J. (1976). *Piaget sampler: An introduction to Jean Piaget through his own words*. New York, NY: Wiley.

Piaget, J. (1989). *The language and thought of the child*. London, England: Routledge.

Piaget, J. (2001). *The psychology of intelligence*. London, England: Routledge.

Piaget, J., & Inhelder, B. (2000). *The psychology of the child*. New York, NY: Basic Books.

Saywitz, K., & Camparo, L. (1998). Interviewing child witnesses: A developmental perspective. *Child Abuse & Neglect, 22*(8), 825–843. doi:10.1016/S0145-2134(98)00054-4

Saywitz, K. J., & Snyder, L. (1996). Narrative elaboration: Test of a new procedure for interviewing children. *Journal of Consulting & Clinical Psychology, 64,* 1347–1357.

Steward, M. S., Bussey, K., Goodman, G. S., & Saywitz, K. J. (1993). Implications of developmental research for interviewing children. *Child Abuse and Neglect, 17*(1), 25–37.

CHAPTER 8

Interviewing to Clarify and Classify Problems

One of the most important functions of assessment is to clarify the nature of the problems that led to the referral in the first place. The assumption is that better understanding the problem will lead to better recommendations for the child and the stakeholders who initiated the referral. This process can take different forms and have different outcomes depending on the context of the assessment. These include gathering the rich personal narrative similar to the Cultural Formulation Interview described in Chapter 6 (DeSilva, Aggarwal, & Lewis-Fernandez, 2015) and/or a formal diagnosis or classification per the *DSM* or the categories of educational disability found in the IDEIA. These two processes can be described as *interviewing for the insider perspective* and *interviewing for diagnosis*. Because the structure of the interview and the approach taken by the assessor are different, I describe them separately in this chapter. At the same time, it is important to understand that in practice they are typically not separate. It is often the case that the assessment starts with gathering information that clarifies the problem from the perspective of the child, parent, or teacher and, if needed, then moves into identifying an appropriate diagnosis or classification.

Interviewing for diagnosis focuses on *nomothetic* information that normally helps the assessor to figure out what kind of person a client is. This is typically expressed in the language of formal classification systems such as the *DSM* or IDEIA. Interviewing for the insider perspective focuses more on *idiographic* information that describes the uniqueness of a person and his or her situation. Again, in the end, these are not mutually exclusive activities although they sometimes need different strategies. For example, interviewing for diagnosis often makes use of highly structured interview protocols, and interviewing for the insider perspective typically uses a more lightly structured interview format and open-ended questions.

Interviewing for the Insider Perspective

As I discuss in Chapter 1, assessment information that lacks the perspective of the stakeholders directly involved in the assessment—for example, teachers, parents, and children themselves—can appear impersonal and disconnected from their original concerns. Attending to the insider perspective makes the assessment process less one-sided and helps build a collaborative relationship as well as provides an ecological check for other assessment information.

Although designed primarily to help English-speaking mental health practitioners interact more effectively with clients from different cultures, the Cultural Formulation Interview (CFI; DeSilva et al., 2015) discussed in Chapter 6 also offers a useful general format for seeking the insider perspective from all our clients. Using the CFI as a base, the process of interviewing for the inside perspective can be conceptualized as having two major components: (1) developing a definition of the problem, including its cause, and (2) understanding efforts at coping and help-seeking.

Definition of the Problem

Murphy (2014) describes the client definition of the problem as the *client position*. Drawing from solution-focused brief therapy and other collaborative approaches to counseling, Murphy describes four steps to discovering the client position that are similar to the steps in the CFI: (1) listening for key words and phrases; (2) exploring clients' opinions about the problem and solution; (3) exploring clients' prior, current, and prospective solutions; and (4) determining what clients want from us and our services (2014, p. 92).

Listening for key words and phrases is an important example of the *skills for not knowing* discussed earlier. These and other skills important for establishing a collaborative relationship are critical for exploring clients' opinions about their problems. In exploring clients' opinions about their problems, whether child, parent, or teacher, it is important not only to make use of the skills for not knowing, but also to avoid arguing or asserting your professional opinion prematurely into the conversation. The assumption is that by not confronting the client's view of the problem, you will avoid provoking greater resistance and obtain a fuller and more accurate picture of how the client views the issue at hand. In the following dialogue, the school counselor is interviewing 14-year-old Barbara:

Practitioner: ***"Hello Barbara. How is it going today?"***
Barbara: ***"Okay I guess. What did you want to talk with me about?"***
Practitioner: ***"Well, your mom called and said that you had stopped taking your medication, and she thought that might be changing your mood. She wanted me to talk with you a little to see what I think about how things are going for you."***
Barbara: ***"The meds make me feel like a zombie! I can't stand feeling that way."***
Practitioner: ***"Okay, wow ... sounds like you really don't like feeling like a zombie ... so, what does that feel like? What I remember is that zombies are dead so I am not sure what they feel." [*****echoing key word, open-ended question*****]***
Barbara: ***"Dead is right ... I am always tired and just feel ... I don't know ... I don't feel anything."***
Practitioner: ***"So, for you the meds make you feel numb ... kind of like you aren't there." [*****reflection*****]***
Barbara: ***[nods and looks down]***
Practitioner: ***"So, I guess when you stop taking your medication, you were trying to solve a problem ... the problem of feeling like a zombie."***
Barbara: ***"Yes ... I don't want to feel that way anymore."***
Practitioner: ***"Okay ... I appreciate that you were really trying to work that out ... how did it work?"***
Barbara: ***"What do you mean?"***
Practitioner: ***"I mean have you stopped feeling dead like a zombie?"***
Barbara: ***"Yes ... I feel alive now but sometimes I get nervous."***
Practitioner: ***"Is that a problem?"***
Barbara: ***"Yes, I can't sleep so much."***
Practitioner: ***"Okay, any other things about not being a zombie that are difficult?"***
Barbara: ***"A little, but that is the biggest one."***

This dialogue shows how by not confronting the client and using the skills for not knowing, including listening for key words and phrases, a practitioner can arrive at a description of the problem from the client's perspective, that is, the client's position. Other information, such as the nature of the medication and what it was being used for, would be important for a more complete assessment, but this information, which is drawn from the practitioner's perspective of what is important, should supplement the client's perspective rather than supplant it.

Coping and Help-Seeking

In addition to understanding the client's opinion about the problem and its causes, it is also important to explore prior, current, and prospective solutions. Exploring past, present, and future attempts to cope with a problem complete our understanding of the *client position*, that is, the client's opinion about the problem, its cause, and what would help.

Better understanding these efforts at coping is also useful in that it focuses us on potential strengths. Saleebey (2008) articulates the basic assumption of the strength perspective:

> First, everyone—every child, every individual, every family, every group, every community and, yes, every teacher and school—has assets, resources, and capacities. There are no exceptions to be made here. Even in the most downtrodden, or most angry, or most defeated of us, there are strengths to be found and nurtured. (p. 69)

From this perspective, we assume that clients, no matter how complex or serious their problems, are working to better their circumstances in some way, even if it is simply to ignore their problems. This focus on clients' assets, as reflected in their attempts to cope, completes the assessment of the insider perspective. The dialogue with Barbara continues:

Practitioner: ***"So, sleep is the biggest thing for you now?"*** ***[*****echo key words*****]***

Barbara: ***[nods]***

Practitioner: ***"So, in the past are there things you have tried to make this better ... to sleep better?"***

Barbara: ***"I guess ... I tried listening to music with earbuds and I tried this breathing thing another counselor taught me a while back."***

Practitioner: ***"Which one worked the best?"***

Barbara: ***"The breathing thing."***

Practitioner: ***"So, are you still doing that now or have you found some other thing that works a little?"*** ***[*****present coping*****]***

Barbara: ***"I still do the breathing sometimes ... it doesn't always work but sometimes."***

Practitioner: ***"Anything you are thinking about doing in the future? Something you think might help a bit."*** ***[*****future coping*****]***

Barbara: ***"My mom says I should take a hot bath at night ... but she is mad at me for not taking my medicine."***

Practitioner: ***"So, you haven't done that but you think it might work?"***

Barbara: ***"Maybe, I like taking baths ... they are really relaxing."***

Practitioner: ***"So, the thing that works about both these things is they help you relax."***

Barbara: ***"Yeah, I think so."***

Practitioner: ***"Well, that is great that you have two things that seem to work a bit. So, on a scale from 1 to 10, how well do you think you are coping with not taking your medicine and not sleeping so well?" [*****use of self-anchored scale to assess overall coping*** *]*

Barbara: ***"Maybe a 6, I'm not sure."***

Practitioner: ***"Wow! A 6 ... I am impressed. I thought for sure you were going to say a 2 or 3. How did you manage that ... making it a 6?"***

Barbara: ***"I don't know ... I guess I really, really don't want to take that medicine."***

Practitioner: ***"I guess you are really determined to find another way to do this."***

Barbara: ***"Determined ... I am not sure what that means."***

Practitioner: ***"Well, it means that when you have a goal or want something you really stick with it."***

Barbara: ***"Oh, my mom says I am stubborn ... is that like the same?"***

Practitioner: ***[laughing] "Yeah, a little bit. In a good way. So, has being stubborn helped you another time that you can think of?"***

Barbara: ***"It helped me when I was learning my times tables when I was younger and when I learned to play the ukulele."***

Practitioner: ***"Gosh, you play the ukulele!"***

Barbara: ***"Yeah ... I saw it on TV and it looked fun."***

Practitioner: ***"Fantastic ... so can I ask you a few questions about the medication so I understand things better?" [*****practitioner transitions to more information about the medication and its uses*** *]*

Barbara: ***"Okay."***

In this dialogue, the practitioner helps Barbara identify strategies she has used to cope with the problem she has identified. The practitioner also helps Barbara to name the strength that seems to underlie her efforts to cope, that is, determination or "being stubborn." After clarifying what the problem is from the client's perspective, that is, the client position, the practitioner begins to move on to gather other information about the problem. The sequence is important in that Barbara may not be interested in solving the problem of not taking her medication, which is the way the adults in her life might frame the problem, but she might be willing to engage in the problem of not sleeping well. In addition, the quality of information about the medication and the reasons for taking the medication will likely be better after spending time understanding Barbara's perspective.

INTERVIEWING FOR DIAGNOSIS AND CLASSIFICATION

Sometimes school-based practitioners have to go beyond identifying the problem from the perspective of the stakeholders who initiate an assessment to identifying the most appropriate formal classification or diagnosis for a client. Human societies have long had ways of classifying the various pains and ills of life, but it is only with the ascension of the scientific method that accurate classification has taken on a special significance as an important tool in the advancement of knowledge (Crotty, 1998). The introduction of the scientific method into medicine has led to a perspective that values precise diagnosis because it assumes a close relationship between diagnosis and treatment. This logic has its origins in the impressive achievements of medicine in combating infectious diseases in the nineteenth and early twentieth centuries (De Jong & Berg, 2013).

Limitations of Diagnosis and Classification

As I discuss in Chapter 1, the logic of the medical model, when applied to mental health problems, has been criticized as being flawed (e.g., De Jong & Berg, 2013; Kamphaus, Dowdy, Kim, & Chin, 2013; Lopez et al., 2006; Sheridan & Gutkin, 2000). Although there are several critiques of the use of classification in mental health and special education, three are especially salient. The first is reliability. The reliability of psychiatric diagnosis has been a concern for decades, and the *DSM* has been offered as a solution with each edition making greater claims for solving the problem (Kirk & Kutchins, 1994). Yet, problems with reliability persist. For example, in field trials for the *DSM-5* (Freedman et al., 2013), interrater reliability was little better than chance for many common diagnoses such as major depressive disorder and generalized anxiety disorder.

In addition, traditional classification systems are rigidly categorical or dichotomous. For example, the two classification systems used by most school-based practitioners, the *DSM* and IDEIA, both assume that a person either has a disorder or disability or does not. There is a strong argument that these categorical approaches do not accurately capture human experience, where the boundaries between normal and psychopathology are not always clear and human characteristics often exist on a continuum rather than in clearly defined categories. A categorical system also leaves no room for students who may have significant functional problems but do not have the specific number of required indicators to be classified as having a disorder or disability (Kamphaus et al., 2013). This last point is especially important in that a *DSM* or IDEIA classification is often required to access needed services.

Another important critique of classifications is their lack of treatment validity (Kamphaus et al., 2013; Timimi, 2014). Simply put, knowing someone's classification or the name of his or her disorder appears to be of only limited value in deciding on a treatment or intervention.

There is limited evidence that treatments, both psychosocial and psychopharmacological, are disorder specific (Timimi, 2014). In other words, an intervention such as using self-talk to help cope with distress or positive reinforcement from a teacher is not specifically tied to a particular disorder but is rather helpful for a variety of different problems.

Despite these critiques, the use of diagnoses (either *DSM* or IDEIA) continues to be pervasive in both community and school settings. Although school-based practitioners must be familiar with these critiques, it is important that they also be thoroughly familiar with diagnostic schemas such as the *DSM* and IDEIA and their use. This allows communication with other mental health professionals and, more importantly, sometimes classification allows children access to needed services (Whitcomb & Merrell, 2013). The rest of this chapter will focus in more depth on these systems and good practices for interviewing for classification.

Framework of the *DSM-5*

Psychoanalytic theory heavily influenced the first two editions of the *DSM*. Starting with *DSM-III*, this was replaced by an atheoretical and descriptive approach to classification (Tsou, 2016). This approach continued with later versions of the *DSM*, including the current *DSM-5* (American Psychiatric Association [APA], 2013). The descriptive approach taken by the *DSM* was motivated by the goal of making diagnoses more reliable and to allow its use by clinicians of different theoretical orientations (Tsou, 2016).

Prior *DSM*s conceptualized disorders as having five dimensions or axes. Axis I included all disorders except intellectual disabilities and personality disorders, which were placed in Axis II. Axis III included medical or health conditions that might co-occur with the primary disorder, and Axis IV included psychosocial stresses or circumstances that contributed to the disorder in some way. Lastly, Axis V consisted of a global assessment of functioning or impairment. The *DSM-5* has moved to a nonaxial system of documentation that combines Axis III with Axes I and II. Instead of formally noting contextual factors such as medical conditions or social stresses on an axis, clinicians first make a diagnosis of a disorder, and then make separate notations for contextual factors and level of disability (APA, 2013).

The *DSM-5* has definitions for 221 disorders, organized into 20 categories (Blashfield & Fuller, 2016). Obviously, no one can be an expert on all 20 categories and 221 disorders. Despite this, it is important for school-based practitioners to be familiar with those disorders they are most likely to encounter in their work. These might include neurodevelopmental disorders such as *autism spectrum disorder*, which occurs in over 1% of the population (APA, 2013), or *attention-deficit/hyperactivity disorder*, which can occur in over 8% of children (APA, 2013). Internalizing disorders such as depression or anxiety are also common, especially as children enter adolescence. Estimated prevalence rates for internalizing disorders vary quite a bit, but an estimate provided by the Centers for Disease Control is 3% for children age 3 to 17 years for both depression and anxiety (Perou et al., 2013), although other estimates are as high as 6% to 8% (Whitcomb & Merrell, 2013).

FRAMEWORK OF IDEIA

In 1975, the U.S. Congress passed the Education for All Handicapped Children Act (EHA). Also known as P.L. 94-142, the purpose of the EHA was to ensure that all children with disabilities had access to a free and appropriate public education that included special education and related services that were designed to meet their unique needs. The law also established procedural safeguards or protections for the rights of children and disabilities and their parents. Prior to P.L. 94-142, over 1 million children with disabilities were completely excluded from public schools, and over half of all children with disabilities had only limited access to a public education (United States Department of Education, n.d.). Given this, the overarching goal of P.L. 94-142 was to improve access.

Congress has amended the EHA several times and reauthorized it in 2004 as the Individuals with Disabilities Education Improvement Act (IDEIA). IDEIA has quite a bit to say about assessment. The most salient points are contained in *Sec. 300.304 Evaluation Procedures* (IDEIA, 2004) and were summarized by Hass and Carriere (2013) as follows:

1. The evaluation should be comprehensive.
2. The evaluator should use a variety of evaluation tools or approaches that gather functional and relevant data.
3. The evaluation should be fair.
4. The evaluator should be competent.
5. The procedures used should be valid and reliable.

These guidelines for assessment are in the service of identifying children with 13 different disabilities:

1. Autism
2. Deaf-blindness
3. Deafness
4. Emotional disturbance
5. Hearing impairment
6. Intellectual disability
7. Multiple disabilities

8. Orthopedic impairment
9. Other health impairments
10. Specific learning disability
11. Speech or language impairment
12. Traumatic brain injury
13. Visual impairment

In my experience, practitioners discuss the categories of IDEIA as if they were altogether different from the medical system of the *DSM*. They are better described as having some differences, but also important similarities. One important difference is that IDEIA is a legal document, whereas the *DSM* is a professional consensus at a point in time. Another important difference is that an individual practitioner can make a *DSM* diagnosis, whereas the establishment of an educational disability is typically a team decision. Lastly, the *DSM* offers more concrete guidelines for making decisions about classification than IDEIA does.

At the same time, the two systems are conceptually very similar. For example, like the *DSM*, the disabilities of IDEIA are categorical. As described earlier, in both systems, a child has a disorder or disability or not, and there is little flexibility or room for nuance in describing a child's problems. Most importantly, both systems play important roles in the identification of categories of *disorder* and *disability* recognized by the government and the medical establishment that lead to needed services (Sherry, 2016).

Making a Differential Diagnosis

Whitcomb and Merrell (2013) describe the process of making a differential diagnosis as having two steps. The first is to decide if the behaviors in question are typical or atypical. For example, symptoms of depression following the death of a family member would be troublesome but not necessarily atypical. Indicators of depression in the absence of acute life stresses would not be typical. Whitcomb and Merrell's (2013) second step is to decide what is the most accurate and fairest way to classify the problem. No matter the classification system (e.g., *DSM*, IDEIA, etc.), these decisions are not about an individual child but rather about a child in a social, cultural, and even historical context. In addition, answering these questions is more difficult the farther the client is from the obvious boundaries of a disorder (Bower, 1982). In other words, there are children whose symptoms are so severe and obvious that we would come to an easy consensus that their behavior is atypical and that they have a certain disorder or disability. Conversely, there are children whose behaviors are so obviously typical, we would all agree that they do not have a problem. Many of the children we deal with are not so obvious, thus making a differential diagnosis less certain and more difficult.

Building on Whitcomb and Merrell's (2013) two-step approach to differential diagnosis, I propose a three-step approach:

1. What symptoms or behaviors are of concern?
2. Are these behaviors typical or atypical?
3. What is the most accurate and fairest classification of the problem?

In medicine, *symptoms* are experiences that people have that are reported rather than observed because they are not directly visible to someone else. This might include pain or feelings of sadness, for example. In contrast, *signs* are observable indicators of a problem such as limping when you walk or not being able to sit still during an interview. School-based practitioners are more familiar with the term *behaviors* rather than *signs*. Given this, in the next section, I will refer to *symptoms* and *problem behaviors*.

STEPS IN DIFFERENTIAL DIAGNOSIS

Step 1 — What Symptoms or Behaviors Are of Concern?

Identifying what symptoms or problem behaviors are of concern is often described as the first step in the problem-solving process (Hurwitz, Gaebler, & Kratochwill, 2007). When done from a behavioral perspective, this stage of the interview seeks to identify and prioritize the symptoms or problems in observable and measurable terms. When the goal is to arrive at a formal diagnosis or classification, it is also valuable to arrive at as specific a description as possible. The strategies and processes are like those described earlier in *interviewing for the insider perspective*. Returning to Barbara:

Practitioner: ***"Fantastic ... so can I ask you a few questions about the medication so I understand things better?" [*practitioner transitions to more information about the medication and its uses*]***
Barbara: ***"Okay."***
Practitioner: ***"May I ask what medication you were taking?"***
Barbara: ***"Okay ... I think it was called pax something."***
Practitioner: ***"Paxil?"***
Barbara: ***"Yeah, that's it."***
Practitioner: ***"So, how come you were taking that?"***
Barbara: ***"I don't know ... my mom says I was really nervous and cranky."***
Practitioner: ***"Nervous? What was that like?"***

Barbara: ***"Well, I guess I was uptight and scared of things. I snapped at my mom a lot and didn't really want to go out because I was nervous something would happen to me or her if I wasn't there ... I also had a lot of stomach aches."***
Practitioner: ***"So, let me see if I got this right ... you were uptight and cranky, nervous about going out and had lots of stomach aches ... anything else?"***
Barbara: ***"I guess I didn't sleep so well before either ... I stayed up worrying a lot."***
Practitioner: ***"What did you worry about?"***
Barbara: ***"I don't know ... everything!"***
Practitioner: ***"Okay, so we will add sleep and worry to our list, okay?"***
Barbara: ***"Yeah ... I guess that is about it."***
Practitioner: ***"Which of those things bother you the most?"***
Barbara: ***"I think the worrying at night and not sleeping."***
Practitioner: ***"Wow, so you were having trouble sleeping before you took the medication and also had trouble after you took the medication. What about the worrying when you were taking the medication?"***
Barbara: ***"I am not sure, maybe that was better a little."***

Barbara's concerns at this point consist of being nervous and cranky, worrying, and having difficulty sleeping. Her priorities focus on worrying and not sleeping. The next step in the process is to establish if these behaviors are typical or atypical.

Step 2—Are These Behaviors Typical or Atypical?

Deciding if a behavior is typical or atypical can be viewed from different perspectives. One is to decide if the behavior is typical or atypical for the client's age or stage of development (Wilmshurst, 2015). For example, tantrums might be typical for a 2-year-old child (depending on frequency and intensity) but less so for a 10-year-old. Although the decline in parent–child relationships during adolescence is overblown, it would not be unusual for a teenager to question unilateral parent authority more than a younger child (Lamb, Hwang, Ketterlinus, & Fracasso, 1999). Yet, having daily intense arguments would not be typical teenage behavior.

To understand whether behavior is typical or atypical from a developmental perspective, it is important to not only look at the child's behavior from the perspective of the expectations of a certain stage of development, but also consider the consequences of such behaviors later in development (Achenbach & Edelbrock, 1984). For example, if it continued, chronic resistance of adult authority could impair a child's ability to function successfully in a classroom later in development. It is possible that Barbara's symptoms of worry and crankiness will disrupt her ability to successfully establish the peer relationships important during adolescence.

In addition to developmental appropriateness, the extent or weight of the symptoms and problem behaviors must also be considered. This includes the number of symptoms or problem behaviors, how often they occur, how long they last when they occur, and in what settings they happen (Wilmshurst, 2015). It is also important to know if things are getting worse, getting better, or staying the same. We know that Barbara is concerned about feeling nervous and cranky, worrying, and having difficulty sleeping but do not yet know the parameters of these symptoms and behaviors. Next, the practitioner explores these with Barbara to understand better if they are typical or atypical.

Practitioner: ***"So, Barbara, you said that you are having trouble sleeping, you feel nervous and cranky and worry a lot. Can I ask you some questions about all that?"***

Barbara: ***"Sure, go ahead."***

Practitioner: ***"When did all this seem to start?" [*how long have the problems existed*]***

Barbara: ***"Not sure, maybe beginning of last semester."***

Practitioner: ***"It is now March, so about 5 or 6 months?***

Barbara: ***"Yeah, it wasn't that bad at first but it has gotten worse since then." [*things are getting worse*]***

Practitioner: ***"I know it may be hard to say but how often during a day do you think you have these feelings?" [*frequency*]***

Barbara: ***"I don't know really. It seems like all the time but it is worse at night."***

Practitioner: ***"So, more or less all the time but maybe a bit less during the day. How come you think it is a little better during the day?" [*settings; note that the practitioner asks about when it is better before asking about when they are worse*]***

Barbara: ***"I think because I am busy during the day and at night nothing much is happening. I am usually just home because I don't feel like going out."***

Practitioner: ***"Okay … being busy may help and not being busy may make things worse, right?"***

Barbara: ***"Think so, yeah"***

Practitioner: ***"Last question for now, okay? If your mom was here and I asked her what this all looked like to her, what would she say?" [*relationship question*]***

Barbara: ***"She is worried … I don't know … she notices I am cranky for sure. I tell her sometimes that I am worried but she doesn't really see it I guess. She knows I don't sleep well. That's why she made me go to the doctor for the medications."***

Practitioner: ***"Okay, I see. So she doesn't see everything but sees enough to be worried about you."***

Barbara: ***"Yes ... she worries too much, too ... " [smiles]***
Practitioner: ***"Maybe she knows what this feels like for herself."***
Barbara: ***"Yeah, maybe."***

At this point, the practitioner knows that from Barbara's perspective (a) the problems have been ongoing for about five or six months; (b) they occur most of the time during the day but seem worse at night; and (c) they also seem to have grown worse since they began at the beginning of the last semester. It is also noteworthy that at least some of the symptoms are serious enough to be visible to her mother. In addition, the last part of the conversation hinted that Barbara's mother might have similar problems.

Another way to examine the weight of symptoms is to consider normative data. Norm-based comparison is the approach used by most behavior rating scales. These types of instruments communicate where a child stands in comparison to his or her peers, and the assumption is that the farther away from the "norm" or mean score, the stronger the evidence is that the behavior in question is more intense and thus more atypical. For example, if Barbara had a *t* score of 76 on the anxiety scale of the Behavior Assessment for Children Self Report of Personality, Third Edition (BASC-3; Reynolds & Kamphaus, 2015), we can assume she views herself as having more symptoms of anxiety than typical and that these symptoms are probably more serious or intense. One approach that I have found useful is to use an instrument like the BASC-3 as the basis for conducting a diagnostic interview. Using the BASC-3 example, this would mean simply using the questions that compose the anxiety scale as prompts to gather more information. For example, the practitioner might ask Barbara, "When you filled out that questionnaire I gave you the other day, you said you worried 'all the time.' Can you tell me a bit more about what you meant?"

Another contribution to the judgment of whether symptoms or behaviors are typical or atypical is the extent to which those difficulties cause impairment in daily life. Impairment in daily life is a requirement for the large majority of diagnoses in the *DSM* (Fabiano & Pelham, 2009). In IDEIA (2004), the phrase "adversely affects educational performance" is standard language in the definitions of the 13 disabilities defined in federal law. Despite this, it is common for practitioners to focus on the indications of a disorder or disability and neglect to assess systematically the extent to which these symptoms have interfered with clients' lives (Lewandowski, Lovett, & Gordon, 2009). This is unfortunate in that indicators of psychopathology appear to have only a moderate correlation with impairment (Angold, Costello, Farmer, Burns, & Erkanli, 1999; Bird et al., 1996). Given this, it is not surprising that other studies have found that when the criterion of impairment is considered carefully, the rates for the diagnoses of mental health problems such as attention-deficit/hyperactivity disorder go down significantly (Bird et al., 1996; Shaffer et al., 1996).

When interviewing for a differential diagnosis, it is important to consider subjective or *phenomenological impairment* as well as *functional impairment in daily life* (Fabiano & Pelham, 2009). These two aspects of impairment are again intertwined, but for the purposes of interviewing for assessment is it important to consider impairment as both a psychological and a social experience (Sherry, 2016).

A comprehensive examination of whether a child's behaviors are typical or atypical should consider if the phenomena in question are troubling to the child him or herself. *Phenomenological impairment* can be understood as the extent to which a client is distressed by the symptoms and behaviors being discussed. Distress has been found to be an important characteristic of a subgroup of internalizing disorders that include depression and generalized anxiety disorder (Eaton, Rodriguez-Seijas, Carragher, & Krueger, 2015), but could easily be a component of many different problems. The distress associated with these disorders can cause impairment in thinking (e.g., attention, worry, loss of vitality or energy, etc.) and difficulties meeting the obligations of school or work or withdrawal from social relationships and positive activities. To understand phenomenological impairment, it is necessary to return to the notion of interviewing for the insider perspective discussed earlier and the process of discovering the meanings children and adolescents give to their life difficulties. We continue our conversation with Barbara:

Practitioner: ***"Barbara ... tell me a bit more about how all this has affected you."*** **[conversational prompt]**

Barbara: ***"Like I said, I don't go out as much as I did. I don't know ... I just like to stay home. It feels better."***

Practitioner: ***"About how often in a week did you used to do things and how often now?"***

Barbara: ***"Maybe two or three times a week before and ... well, not really at all anymore."***

Practitioner: ***"So, what keeps you from going out?"***

Barbara: ***"I don't know ... I just get nervous and it feels safer at home."***

Practitioner: ***"On a scale of 1 to 10—with 10 being total panic and 1 being total chill—how would you rate yourself lately?"*** **[note use of scaling questions]**

Barbara: ***"Don't know ... maybe an 8 ... it gets pretty bad I guess."***

Practitioner: ***"Okay, so an 8, which sounds like a lot of nervousness."***

Barbara: ***"Yeah."***

Practitioner: ***"So what is that 8 like? What's it like inside your head and body?"***

Barbara: ***"I just feel all uptight and my mind is racing ... like I can't keep up with my thoughts. Then it's hard to concentrate ... I feel like I have ADD. It is hard to listen and I feel like I have get up and move around ... like I can't sit still."***

Practitioner: ***"Wow … that sounds like a lot."***

Barbara: ***[starts to tear up] "I don't let many people know but I feel like crap all the time."***

Practitioner: ***"This is hard stuff, Barbara. Let's see what we can do to make things better. I have a few more questions, though … would that be okay?"***

At this point, the practitioner has gained some knowledge of Barbara's sense of phenomenological impairment. We know that on a scale of 1 to 10, she experiences herself as having quite a lot of nervousness (8 out of 10). We also know that she experiences her mind as racing and has difficulty concentrating. The next step is to understand how this has affected her socially and academically. It is important to understand that impairment is both a personal and a social experience in that it can reflect the perceived failure of clients to live up to the developmental, academic, and social expectations of the families, schools, and communities where they live (Sherry, 2016). Fabiano and Pelham (2009) argue that children typically present with difficulties in the domains of (a) peer relationships, (b) adult relationships, and (c) academic achievement. In the following dialogue with Barbara, the practitioner systematically explores each of these domains:

Practitioner: ***"Okay, is it okay if we go a bit further with these questions?"***

Barbara: ***"Okay."***

Practitioner: ***"How are things going with your friends?" [*peers*]***

Barbara: ***"Like I said, I don't go out very much. I still text them some but none of them call or anything. I guess they just think I sorta disappeared."***

Practitioner: ***"Compared to before, you are not seeing your friends very much?"***

Barbara: ***"No, not much. I used to go out a lot more."***

Practitioner: ***"How about with adults, like your mom or teachers?" [*adults*]***

Barbara: ***"Well … you know; my mom is worried but she is a worrier. Guess I am like her a bit."***

Practitioner: ***"Okay, but how you getting along?"***

Barbara: ***"Okay I guess … I don't like to talk to her too much about it because she freaks out."***

Practitioner: ***"So, you talk to her less than before?"***

Barbara: ***"Not really I guess, about the same."***

Practitioner: ***"What about your teachers?"***

Barbara: ***"I am missing school a lot because I am tired from not sleeping … I get nervous and just want to stay home I guess."***

Practitioner: ***"When you are there, how's it with them?"***

Barbara: ***"They're nice ... they always ask why I didn't make it to school and give me make-up work."***

Practitioner: ***"That sounds good ... so, you get along pretty well with both your mom and teachers but maybe you don't see your teachers as much and you avoid talking to your mom sometimes because you don't want her to freak out?"***

Barbara: ***"Yeah."***

Practitioner: ***"What about school ... how's your grades?" [*academic achievement*]***

Barbara: ***"They were okay before ... but I'm not sure now. I missed a bunch of school and haven't done much homework."***

Practitioner: ***"Okay, you're not sure but you think it may not be going that well ... we can check on that if you want. So, before, you got pretty good grades .... How did you do, specifically?"***

Barbara: ***"Mostly Bs, sometimes I would get an A ... I like language arts and reading."***

Practitioner: ***"Oh, cool ... do you read at home?"***

Barbara: ***"Yeah, I read a lot of books ... I really like fantasy and science fiction."***

Practitioner: ***"I do too! Seems like the big things are going to school and getting back in the swing of things doing and work."***

Barbara: ***"Yeah, I think so."***

Barbara's problems appear to have had a significant impact on her life. In addition to knowing that she views herself as nervous, which seems to result in her mind racing and having difficulty concentrating, we now also know that she has withdrawn from many social activities, misses school, and does not do her homework as before. Given this and what we learned earlier about the history of her problems with anxiety, the extent to which they occur during the day, and the fact that they seem to be growing worse, it would be a reasonable conclusion that these behaviors are not typical. The next step in the process of making a differential diagnosis is to determine what would be the most accurate and fairest classification of these problems.

Step 3—What Is the Most Accurate and Fairest Classification of These Problems?

Making a diagnosis or classification requires that you have a good understanding of the classification system you are using, for example, *DSM* or IDEIA. It is beyond the scope of this book to go into detail about each of the 13 IDEIA categories or the over 200 disorders in the *DSM*, but some questions follow that can assist practitioners in arriving at an accurate and fair specific diagnosis and, more importantly, a clearer understanding of the client.

First Question — Do These Problems Appear to Be Developmental in Nature?

In the *DSM*, neurodevelopmental disorders are described as disorders that typically manifest "early in development, often before the child enters grade school, and are characterized by developmental deficits that produce impairments of personal, social academic, or occupational functioning" (APA, 2013, p. 31). These impairments usually present as delays in meeting typically occurring developmental milestones such as communication or academic achievement. The specific disorders in the *DSM* (APA, 2013) category of neurodevelopmental disorders include:

1. Intellectual disabilities
2. Communication disorders
3. Autism spectrum disorder
4. Attention-deficit/hyperactivity disorder
5. Specific learning disorder
6. Motor disorder (including Tourette's disorder and other tic disorders)

It is important to note that, with small differences in language, there is a 100% overlap between the preceding neurodevelopmental disorders and many of the disabilities in IDEIA.

The data needed to determine if the problems being discussed are developmental can come from a review of documents such as early school records or developmental histories completed by parents or guardians. It can also come from interviewing parents or clients themselves about when the presenting problems began to emerge. We know from our previous conversation that, at least from Barbara's perspective, these symptoms seemed to have begun about five or six months ago. In any assessment, it is important to confirm this information with other informants. In the following short dialogue between the practitioner and Barbara's mother, the practitioner explores further the onset of Barbara's problems and their possible developmental implications:

Practitioner: ***"Hi Mrs. B., you asked me to talk with Barbara about her medication and I had a couple of questions about some things she said. Can I ask you some questions?"***

Mother: ***"Sure, I am really worried about her. You know she has been missing a lot of school and her grades are going down fast."***

Practitioner: ***"Yeah, that doesn't sound good ... so, she talks about being nervous a lot and not being able to sleep very well. She also says she is crankier than usual. Does that sound about right?"***

Mother: ***"Yes, that's right. I try to keep her calm but she is so easily set off."***

Practitioner: ***"About how long has this been going on?"***
Mother: ***"Maybe six months ... she has always been a little high strung but she was really fine until about six months ago. Then, she started to get really anxious, especially at night. She would wake up tired and then didn't want to go to school. Before that she was always a good student. God knows what her grades are now."***
Practitioner: ***"So, it seemed to come on pretty quickly about six months ago? Before that she might have been high strung but she was doing pretty well?"***
Barbara: ***"Yeah, I hope we can figure out what is going on."***

Although Barbara had always been high-strung, this was not a concern until about six months ago. Taken together, Barbara's and her mother's accounts suggest that her current problems did not manifest early in development are not developmental in nature in the same way that the neurodevelopmental disorders listed earlier are.

Second Question—Are the Client's Problems Primarily Internalizing or Externalizing or a Mix of Both?

The understanding that disorders cluster into two primary dimensions, internalizing and externalizing, goes back several decades (Achenbach & Edelbrock, 1978, 1984). Internalizing problems include depression, anxiety, withdrawal, and somatic symptoms (physical problems in the absence of a known physical illness), whereas externalizing problems include aggression, hyperactivity, defiance, and conduct problems (Whitcomb & Merrell, 2013). Many studies have confirmed these findings (Eaton et al., 2015), and data suggest that these dimensions are stable over time and invariant across gender, ethnicity, age, and sexual orientation (Krueger & Eaton, 2015).

Although the weight of evidence supports these two primary dimensions, some researchers have presented data suggesting that *thought disorders* may be a third dimension (Carragher, Krueger, Eaton, & Slade, 2015).). Thought disorders are often associated with psychotic disorders and include behaviors such as confused thinking, delusions, and hallucinations (APA, 2013; Whitcomb & Merrell, 2013).

Other researchers argue that internalizing disorders can be further reduced to the lower order factors of *distress* (e.g., depression, generalized anxiety, etc.) and *fear* (phobias; Krueger & Markon, 2006). Further analysis of externalizing disorders suggests they can be meaningfully reduced to the lower order factors of *oppositional behavior* (attention-deficit/hyperactivity disorder and oppositional defiant disorder) and *social norm violation* (conduct disorder, antisocial behavior, substance abuse; Farmer, Seeley, Kosty, & Lewinsohn, 2009). Given the strength of these dimensions, it is important for practitioners to consider how the problems noted in Step 1 earlier fit these patterns. The second question of "Are the client's problems primarily internalizing or externalizing or a mix of both?" can be divided into the following four questions:

1. Are the client's problems primarily internalizing or externalizing?
2. If mostly internalizing, is distress or fear the primary issue?
3. If mostly externalizing, are the behaviors more oppositional or conduct?
4. Are there signs of a thought disorder?

As previously noted, Barbara's problems include feeling nervous and cranky, worrying, and having difficulty sleeping. These behaviors appear to be internalizing in nature. Furthermore, they seem to fit the subcategory of distress rather than the specific fears associated with phobias or panic attacks. There is also no sign of a thought disorder.

Third Question — What Diagnosis Best Fits the Information?

Our understanding of Barbara suggests that her problems are not typical for her age and development yet do not appear to be developmental in nature. In addition, they seem to best fit the categories of internalizing and distress. Lastly, there are no signs of a thought disorder. This helps us narrow considerably the possible classifications for Barbara's problems. The following questions help us further narrow down these possibilities.

Question 3a—What Are the Most Likely Possibilities? We have eliminated many of the over 200 possibilities contained in the *DSM* (APA, 2013) and most of the categories in IDEIA. Of the major *DSM* categories, the category of anxiety disorders seems to fit with Barbara's signs and symptoms. In the *DSM* (APA, 2013), anxiety disorders include:

1. Separation anxiety disorder
2. Selective mutism
3. Specific phobia
4. Social phobia
5. Panic disorder
6. Agoraphobia
7. Generalized anxiety disorder

Of these, the phobias and panic disorders do not appear to fit because her problems appear to be more an expression of distress than specific fears. This leaves separation anxiety disorder and generalized anxiety disorder as the most likely candidates for an appropriate diagnosis.

Question 3b—Of These, Which One Seems the Most Likely Given the Evidence? Separation anxiety disorder is characterized by excessive anxiety related to separation from individuals to whom the client is attached (APA, 2013). This does not seem to be the best fit for Barbara's description of what troubles her. This leaves us with generalized anxiety disorder (GAD) as the most likely *DSM* diagnosis. GAD involves excessive worry and includes symptoms such as irritability, sleep disturbance, difficulty concentrating, restlessness, being easily fatigued, and muscle tension (APA, 2013). Three of these symptoms are required, although with children only one is needed. In addition to the presence of these symptoms, the person must experience significant impairment and the symptoms must be present for at least 6 months, more days than not. Barbara appears to meet these criteria, leaving GAD as perhaps the best classification of her symptoms and problem behaviors.

Up to this point, we have discussed Barbara from the perspective of the *DSM*, but the same logic can be applied to the 13 IDEIA categories. Of the 13 disabilities listed in IDEIA, autism, intellectual disability, specific learning disability, and speech or language impairment would be considered developmental in the same way that neurodevelopmental disabilities are in the *DSM*. Deaf-blindness, hearing impairment, orthopedic impairment, traumatic brain injury, and visual impairment can also be ruled out. We can put aside for the moment the category of multiple disabilities because, of course, we should first establish the presence of one disability before determining if there are multiple. This leaves emotional disturbance (ED) and other health impairment (OHI).

In IDEIA (2004), ED is defined as

> (4) (i) *Emotional disturbance* means a condition exhibiting one or more of the following characteristics over a long period of time and to a marked degree that adversely affects a child's educational performance:
>
> A. An inability to learn that cannot be explained by intellectual, sensory, or health factors.
> B. An inability to build or maintain satisfactory interpersonal relationships with peers and teachers.
> C. Inappropriate types of behavior or feelings under normal circumstances.
> D. A general pervasive mood of unhappiness or depression.
> E. A tendency to develop physical symptoms or fears associated with personal or school problems.
>
> (ii) Emotional disturbance includes schizophrenia. The term does not apply to children who are socially maladjusted, unless it is determined that they have an emotional disturbance under paragraph (c)(4)(i) of this section.

Barbara might fit the criteria for "A tendency to develop physical symptoms or fears associated with personal or school problems" if it is decided that the problems she describes significantly impair her ability to function in school and there is a need for special education. Given that she is not doing homework and is absent frequently, there would be an argument for the ED classification. At the same time, it would seem premature to classify her thus and decide that special education is needed without an attempt to provide greater support and high-quality interventions.

OHI is a second IDEIA category that could fit Barbara. OHI is defined as

> (9) *Other health impairment* means having limited strength, vitality, or alertness, including a heightened alertness to environmental stimuli, that results in limited alertness with respect to the educational environment, that —
>
> (i) Is due to chronic or acute health problems such as asthma, attention deficit disorder or attention deficit hyperactivity disorder, diabetes, epilepsy, a heart condition, hemophilia, lead poisoning, leukemia, nephritis, rheumatic fever, sickle cell anemia, and Tourette syndrome; and
>
> (ii) Adversely affects a child's educational performance.

The list of conditions in the definition of OHI is not exhaustive nor does having one of the named conditions automatically qualify a child for special education. The team at Barbara's school might find that her symptoms of anxiety represent a "chronic or acute health problem" but to do so there must be evidence that the symptoms limit "strength, vitality, or alertness." Given her problems sleeping and absences, there appears to be evidence that this could be true. As with ED, there is evidence that her problems adversely affect her educational performance. As with ED, it would seem prudent to provide support in general education before arriving at the decision that she needs special education.

As described, the process of making a differential diagnosis is difficult, and more demanding of a broad set of skills and in-depth knowledge of development and psychopathology (Whitcomb & Merrell, 2013). The process is complicated by the problems with reliability and validity discussed earlier. The goal of the steps and preceding questions is to give school-based practitioners a systematic way of thinking about the process of classification. This process is summarized in Appendix 3.

Conclusion

Although this chapter describes the processes of *interviewing for the insider perspective* and *interviewing for diagnosis* as separate, it again is important to remember that in practice they are intertwined. *Interviewing for the insider perspective* allows practitioners to clarify the concerns that led to the assessment from the perspective of the child, parent, or teacher. It furthers the collaborative relationship before moving to the more specific questions needed to identify an appropriate diagnosis or classification.

Given the limitations of diagnosis or classification, it is best to view it as part of a broader process of case formulation. Taken together, *interviewing for diagnosis* and *interviewing for the insider perspective* can fulfill two of the three steps of Wilmshurst's (2015) three-part model of case formulation: *problem identification* and *problem understanding*. Together, they can better serve the goal of developing the high-quality interventions needed to make a difference in the life of a child.

Chapter 8 Takeaway Points

- Interviewing to understand better a client's problems can involve interviewing for the insider perspective or interviewing for diagnosis.
- Interviewing for the insider perspective involves discovering the client's understanding of the problem and her attempts at coping and help-seeking.
- The process of diagnosis has been criticized for its lack of reliability, categorical structure, and poor treatment validity.
- At the same time, diagnosis is important in community and school settings because it is often required for needed services.
- The categories of the *DSM* and IDEIA are important for school-based practitioners to be familiar with.
- Differential diagnosis can be divided into three steps: (1) What symptoms or behaviors are of concern? (2) Are these behaviors typical or atypical? (3) What is the most accurate and fairest classification of the problem?
- The decision of typical or atypical takes into consideration (a) developmental expectations, (b) weight or extend of problems, and (c) impairment.
- The decisions as to the most accurate and fairest classification can be guided by three further questions: (1) Do these problems appear to be developmental in nature? (2) Are the client's problems primarily internalizing or externalizing or a mix of both? and (3) What diagnosis best fits the information?
- The decision as to what diagnosis best fits the information can be guided by asking, what are the most likely possibilities? and of these, which one seems the most likely given the evidence?

References

Achenbach, T. M., & Edelbrock, C. S. (1978). The classification of child psychopathology: A review and analysis of empirical efforts. *Psychological Bulletin, 85*(6), 1275–1301. doi:10.1037/0033-2909.85.6.1275

Achenbach, T. M., & Edelbrock, C. S. (1984). Psychopathology of childhood. *Annual Review of Psychology, 35*, 227–256.

American Psychiatric Association. (2013). *Diagnostic and statistical manual of mental disorders* (5th ed.). Washington, DC: Author.

Angold, A., Costello, E. J., Farmer, E. M., Burns, B. J., & Erkanli, A. (1999). Impaired but undiagnosed. *Journal of the American Academy of Child and Adolescent Psychiatry, 38*, 129–137.

Bird, H. R., Andrews, H., Schwab-Stone, M., Goodman, S., Dulcan, M., Richters, J., ... Gould, M. S. (1996). Global measures of impairment for epidemiological and clinical use with children and adolescents. *International Journal of Methods in Psychiatric Research, 6*, 295–307.

Blashfield, R. K., & Fuller, A. K. (2016). Predicting the *Diagnostic and statistical manual of mental disorders* (fifth edition): The mystery of how to constrain unchecked growth. *Journal of Nervous and Mental Disease, 204*(6), 415–420. doi:10.1097/NMD.0000000000000491

Bower, E. M. (1982). Defining emotional disturbance: Public policy and research. *Psychology in the Schools, 19*, 55–60.

Carragher, N., Krueger, R. F., Eaton, N. R., & Slade, T. (2015). Disorders without borders: Current and future directions in the meta-structure of mental disorders. *Social Psychiatry and Psychiatric Epidemiology, 50*(3), 339–350. doi:10.1007/s00127-014-1004-z

Crotty, M. (1998). *The foundations of social research: Meaning and perspective in the research process*. London, England: Sage.

De Jong, P., & Berg, I. K. (2013). *Interviewing for solutions*. Belmont, CA: Brooks/Cole, Cengage Learning.

DeSilva, R., Aggarwal, N. K., & Lewis-Fernandez, R. (2015, June 30). The *DSM-5* Cultural Formulation Interview and the evolution of cultural assessment in psychiatry. *Psychiatric Times*.

Eaton, N. R., Rodriguez-Seijas, C., Carragher, N., & Krueger, R. F. (2015). Transdiagnostic factors of psychopathology and substance use disorders: A review. *Social Psychiatry & Psychiatric Epidemiology, 50*(2), 171–182. doi:10.1007/s00127-014-1001-2

Fabiano, G. A., & Pelham, W. J. (2009). Impairment in children. In S. Goldstein & J. A. Naglieri (Eds.), *Assessing impairment: From theory to practice* (pp. 105–119). New York, NY: Springer Science. doi:10.1007/978-0-387-87542-2_9

Farmer, R., Seeley, J., Kosty, D., & Lewinsohn, P. (2009). Refinements in the hierarchical structure of externalizing psychiatric disorders: Patterns of lifetime liability from mid-adolescence through early adulthood. *Journal of Abnormal Psychology, 118*(4), 699–710.

Freedman, R., Lewis, D., Michels, R., Pine, D., Schultz, S., Tamminga, C., ... Yager, J. (2013). The initial field trials of *DSM-5*: New blooms and old thorns. *American Journal of Psychiatry, 170*(1), 1–5. doi:10.1176/appi.ajp.2012.12091189

Hass, M., & Carriere, J. A. (2013). *Writing useful, accessible, and legally defensible psychoeducational reports*. Hoboken, NJ: Wiley.

Hurwitz, J. T., Gaebler, E. R., & Kratochwill, T. R. (2007). Dealing with school systems and teachers. In M. Hersen & J. C. Thomas (Eds.), *Handbook of clinical interviewing with children* (pp. 95–114). Thousand Oaks, CA: Sage. doi:10.4135/9781412982740.n7

Individuals with Disabilities Education Improvement Act, Pub. L. No. 108-446, 118 Stat. 2647 (2004).

Kamphaus, R. W., Dowdy, E., Kim, S., & Chin, J. (2013). Diagnosis, classification, and screening systems. In D. H. Saklofske, V. L. Schwean, & C. R. Reynolds (Eds.), *The Oxford handbook of child psychological assessment* (pp. 182–201). doi:10.1093/oxfordhb/9780199796304.013.0009

Kirk, S. A., & Kutchins, H. (1994). The myth of the reliability of *DSM*. *Journal of Mind and Behavior, 15*(1–2), 71–86.

Krueger, R., & Eaton, N. (2015). Transdiagnostic factors of mental disorders. *World Psychiatry, 14*(1), 27–29.

Krueger R. F., & Markon, K. E. (2006). Reinterpreting comorbidity: A model-based approach to understanding and classifying psychopathology. *Annual Review in Clinical Psychology, 2*, 111–133.

Lamb, M. E., Hwang, C. P., Ketterlinus, R. D., & Fracasso, M. P. (1999). Parent–child relationships: Development in the context of the family. In M. H. Bornstein & M. E. Lamb (Eds.), *Developmental psychology: An advanced textbook* (4th ed., pp. 411–450). Mahwah, NJ: Erlbaum.

Lewandowski, L. J., Lovett, B. J., & Gordon, M. (2009). Measurement of symptom severity and impairment. In S. Goldstein & J. A. Naglieri (Eds.), *Assessing impairment: From theory to practice* (pp. 5–14). New York, NY: Springer Science. doi:10.1007/978-0-387-87542-2_2

Lopez, S. J., Edwards, L. M., Pedrotti, J. T., Prosser, E. C., LaRue, S., Spalitto, S. V., & Ulven, J. C. (2006). Beyond the *DSM-IV*: Assumptions, alternatives, and alterations. *Journal of Counseling & Development, 84*(3), 259–267. doi:10.1002/j.1556-6678.2006.tb00404.x

Murphy, J. J. (2014). *Solution-focused counseling in schools* (2nd ed.). Alexandria, VA: American Counseling Association.

Perou, R., Bitsko, R. H., Blumberg, S. J., Pastor, P., Ghandour, R. M., Gfroerer, J. C., ... Huang, L. N. (2013). Mental health surveillance among children—United States, 2005–2011. *MMWR: Morbidity & Mortality Weekly Report*, 621–635.

Reynolds, C. R., & Kamphaus, R. W. (2015). *Behavior assessment system for children* (3rd ed.). San Antonio, TX: Pearson.

Saleebey, D. (2008). Commentary on the strengths perspective and potential applications in school counseling. *Professional School Counseling, 12*(2), 68–75.

Shaffer, D., Fisher, P., Dulcan, M. K., Davies, M., Piacentini, J., Schwab-Stone, M., ... Regier, D. A. (1996). The NIMH Diagnostic Interview Schedule for Children version 2.3: I. Description, acceptability, prevalence rates, and performance in the MECA study. *Journal of the American Academy of Child and Adolescent Psychiatry, 35*, 865–877.

References

Sheridan, S. M., & Gutkin, T. B. (2000). The ecology of school psychology: Examining and changing our paradigm for the 21st century. *School Psychology Review, 29*(4), 485–502.

Sherry, M. (2016). A sociology of impairment. *Disability & Society, 31*(6), 729–744. doi: 10.1080/09687599.2016.1203290

Timimi, S. (2014). No more psychiatric labels: Why formal psychiatric diagnostic systems should be abolished. *International Journal of Clinical and Health Psychology, 14,* 208–215. doi:10.1016/j.ijchp.2014.03.004

Tsou, J. Y. (2016). Natural kinds, psychiatric classification and the history of the *DSM*. *History of Psychiatry, 27*(4), 406–424. doi:10.1177/0957154X16656580

United States Department of Education, Office of Special Education Programs. (n.d.). *History: Twenty-five years of progress in educating children with disabilities through IDEA*. Retrieved July 24, 2017, from https://www2.ed.gov/policy/speced/leg/idea/history.html

Whitcomb, S. A., & Merrell, K. W. (2013). *Behavioral, social, and emotional assessment of children and adolescents* (4th ed.). New York, NY: Routledge.

Wilmshurst, L. (2015). *Child and adolescent psychopathology: A casebook* (3rd ed.). Thousand Oaks, CA: Sage.

CHAPTER 9

Interviewing About Academic Performance

This chapter focuses on interviewing children when their academic performance is the primary concern. Academic performance is always an important issue for school-based practitioners and they are in a unique position to offer useful information to teachers and parents about the acquisition of academic skills or improving classroom behavior. Academic skills are often assessed using standardized tests. Although useful in many ways, the results of a test do not tell us what children experience when they try to read or solve math problems. By themselves, they also do not necessarily offer the kind of information needed to change instruction or decide goals.

In interviewing children about academic performance, the first step is to ask about the student's likes and dislikes at school, experiences doing homework, and their relationship toward teachers. Additional questions might include asking students if they think they understand the assignment, feel confident about completing the assignment, or think they have enough time to complete it (Shapiro, 2011). A second step draws upon Ginsburg's use of *clinical interviews* in research on mathematical thinking (Ginsburg, 1981, 1997; Ginsburg, Lee, & Pappas, 2016) and *curriculum-based assessment* (Deno, 1992). In addition, we will discuss interviewing teachers about their students' academic performance.

Clinical Interviews as Applied to Academic Learning

Piaget pioneered the use of clinical interviews in his research on children's thinking and cognitive development (Ginsburg, 1981). Ginsburg (1997) argues that clinical interviews have significant advantages over either standardized tests or naturalistic observations, if the goal is to understand how children think about the problems they solve. The clinical interview starts with a task followed by open-ended questions, which ask children to think aloud about how they solved an academic task and why they used the strategies they used (Ginsburg, 1981). In addition, assessments of academic performance often rely heavily on tests or information provided by teachers and do not account for the experience of the child. Clinical interviews of academic performance correct for this and offer information about the insider perspective discussed earlier.

Although clinical interviews have primarily been used to study children's performance in math, it is a strategy that has potential utility for other subjects, such as reading or written language. Similar strategies come from approaches to literacy instruction. For example, in the Reading Recovery Program (Clay, 2005), reading teachers are encouraged to observe and analyze what students are doing when they read, often using questions that probe underlying strategies and processes. This includes listening to how the reading sounds and observing what the student does well or easily and what is difficult (Lipp & Helfrich, 2016). Fried (2013) describes three aspects to this process, including making note of (1) *tolds* (times when the teacher or assessor tells students the word); (2) performance on high-frequency words; and (3) self-monitoring or problem-solving activities that lead to self-correction. Like clinical interviews, Reading Recovery encourages the teacher to ask students if they are correct or not, and to question how they know this (Clay, 2005), thus getting at the thinking that underlies the performance.

As noted earlier, clinical interviews of academic performance start with a task. Curriculum-based assessment gives a framework for choosing these tasks. Deno (1992) distinguishes curriculum-based assessment (CBA) from curriculum-based measurement (CBM). CBA is a general term that refers to approaches that gather information on academic performance using the actual curriculum (Deno, 1992; Shinn, 2002). CBM refers to one type of CBA that uses short standardized tests of basic skills to assess placement in the curriculum and measure progress (Shinn, 2002). In the context of interviewing for assessment, the focus is on the more general forms of CBA that lend themselves to task and subskill analysis (Deno, 1992). CBA can take the form of teacher-generated tests, worksheets, and permanent products. Choosing a task can be as simple as asking the child to bring a relevant work sample to the interview or asking the teacher to provide an appropriate text or worksheet.

In the following interview, a school psychologist interviews 8-year-old Amy about reading. In the interview, the school psychologist starts with a modification of the Typical Day Interview and questions about her perceived strengths and challenges. It moves from there into the use of CBA and elements of clinical interviewing as discussed earlier.

Practitioner: ***"Hi Amy, my name is Miss Nancy. You are in Mrs. Serrano's class, right?"***

Amy: ***"Yes, I am in second grade."***

Practitioner: ***"Okay.... So, when you get to school what is the first thing you do?"*** *[***classroom-focused typical day interview***]*

Amy: ***"First we do attendance ... then the teacher reads part of the story we are reading. Then we do reading and writing, later we do math. In the afternoon, we do science or social studies."***

Practitioner: ***"Okay, what is your favorite—reading, writing, math, science, or social studies?"***

Amy: ***"First social studies, then math and science ... last is writing and reading."***

Practitioner: ***"Oh, what do you like about social studies or math?"***

Amy: ***"I like the stories in social studies about things that happened a long time ago. Math ... I am good at math." [smiles]***

Practitioner: ***"That's fantastic Amy ... what about reading?"***

Amy: ***"I don't know ... I'm slow ... the other kids read faster."***

Practitioner: ***"Oh, so it is like you don't have enough time to finish reading something?"***

Amy: ***"No, everyone finishes before me."***

Practitioner: ***"If you have enough time, can you read everything?"***

Amy: ***"I don't know, maybe."***

Practitioner: ***"So, when you read it is slow ... okay ... I was wondering if you could read a little bit with me, and we can see if we can figure some things out. How about we use this book your teacher gave me? Okay?"*** *[***introduction to clinical interviewing task***]*

Amy: ***"Okay ... " [Amy begins to read from the book. She reads slowly, pausing to deliberately sound out several words.]***

Practitioner: ***[after a few minutes] "Okay Amy, thanks. Can I ask you some questions about reading?"***

Amy: ***"Okay."***

Practitioner: ***"Well, what part was easy and what part was hard?"***

Amy: ***"These words are easy." [Amy points to some of the words that she recognizes by sight and does not need to sound out.]***

Practitioner: ***"Okay, can we read a few of them again?" [Amy reads a few words.] "Okay, great. It seems you just know those words and you don't have to think about them too much."***

Amy: ***"Yeah ... I remember them easy."***

Practitioner: ***"So, which ones are hard then?"***
Amy: ***"The words like this one." [Amy points to a word she had to sound out slowly.]***
Practitioner: ***"Oh, that one is hard ... okay, what is hard about it?"***
Amy: ***"I don't know ... I have to sound it out."***
Practitioner: ***"Okay, let's try a few of them again to see how you do." [Amy reads a few of the words, again sounding out each one slowly.] "Okay, Amy what is the sound that this letter makes?" [Practitioner points to a series of letters and Amy makes the sound.] "Okay ... Amy it seems you know the sounds of all those letters but when you try to put them together it gets hard ... does that sound right?"***
Amy: ***"I guess, I can do it but I am slower than the other girls."***
Practitioner: ***"Okay, thanks Amy ... I am going to talk with your teacher and we will see if we can get you some more help learning to do that faster, okay?"***
Amy: ***"Okay ... can I go back to class now?"***
Practitioner: ***"Sure, we can talk more later."***

In this interview, the school psychologist has learned that Amy likes social studies and perceives herself as good at math. She also often feels she doesn't have enough time to finish reading what she needs to read to complete an assignment. Further evidence of this comes out in the clinical interview/CBA part of the interview as Amy reads slowly and seems to have difficulty with words she needed to decode.

Interviewing Teachers and Parents About Academic Performance

In schools, teachers are often the ones who initiate referrals for assessment, making them critical informants in the assessment process. This is especially true when the reason for the referral is focused on academic achievement. The general strategies for interviewing teachers are the same as the strategies used for interviewing students (McConaughy, 2013). This includes the stance of not knowing (Anderson & Goolishian, 1992) and the skills for developing a collaborative relationship (e.g., nonverbal skills, verbal skills, question strategies and prompts, etc.) discussed in Chapter 4. Interviewing teachers also makes use of the five steps discussed in Chapter 3:

1. Develop a focus by thinking through the goals and topics beforehand.
2. Open with introductions, small talk, and a yes set.
3. Make a transitional structuring statement.
4. Transition to specific interview questions or topics.
5. Close the interview.

Step 1 involves thinking through the topics and subtopics for an interview. The first topic is exploring the reasons that led to the referral and arriving at a definition of the problem. For teachers, this involves understanding what the problem is, what they believe is causing the problem, what they have tried to do about the problem prior to referring the student for an assessment, and what they think would help, that is, what they want from the assessment.

Because teacher interviews often focus on academic performance, more specific topics include getting details about students' performance in each of the main academic areas of reading, written language, and mathematics. It is important to try to determine the relative impacts of academic achievement and the ability to demonstrate those skills in the classroom. For example, a student with a specific learning disability may have difficulties with skill acquisition, which then hinders his performance in the classroom. A student who is depressed or perhaps has attention-deficit/hyperactivity disorder may have excellent academic skills but have difficulty demonstrating those skills in classroom assignments. This distinction is critical in the assessment process for arriving at interventions.

One source of information about academic skill is group assessments such as those required by the state or federal government and through district- or school-level benchmark testing. These provide limited information but could be considered a starting point in conversations with teachers.

Understanding students' academic skills often involves comparisons—to other students, to state or school district standards, to other children in the class, or to what might be expected by someone of the same grade and background. When making these comparisons, it is useful to consider both the *level* of achievement and the *rate* of growth. Comparisons are not only with other children or to external standards but can also be within the person—for example, how a student performs in math versus how he performs in reading. Probing further, we are also interested in how students perform in one aspect of an academic area versus another, for example, reading words versus reading comprehension or paper and pencil math calculation versus applied math, and so on. When interviewing teachers, questions might include:

- How does Michael's performance compare with the average student in your class?
- How fast is he learning the material compared to other students in your class?
- How did he do the last time you did benchmark testing?
- How well did he do on the last state testing? Do you have those records?
- Can we break down reading a bit? For example, how does he do in reading words versus reading comprehension? How about math? Does he do better in math calculation or word problems?

Academic performance is, of course, closely connected to academic skills. For example, someone may not pay attention during a lesson because he does not understand or have the skills to take part, or she may have adequate academic skills but lack the ability to focus on the lesson. The first step in unpacking this is to ask about students' behavior when engaged in a certain academic activity (Shapiro, 2011). These questions might include:

- How does John behave during reading?
- When you ask Mary to read aloud, what does she do?
- When she is doing independent math, does Justine seem engaged and on task?

Other aspects of academic performance include the ability to follow classroom routines, work cooperatively with others, listen during group instruction, and so on. In addition, it is useful to ask teachers what interventions or accommodations they have tried and how effective these were. As with exceptions (De Shazer, 1988), these attempts at solutions often hold clues to interventions, even if they have not been completely successful. The following dialogue between a school counselor and Mrs. Martinez, a second-grade teacher, illustrates some of the topics and questions discussed earlier. Mrs. Martinez has referred Mary for an assessment because she is falling behind her peers in reading and is being considered for retention.

Practitioner: ***"Hi, Mrs. Martinez, thanks for taking the time to meet with me. Can you start by just telling me a little bit about Mary?"*** **[open-ended prompt]**

Mrs. Martinez: ***"Sure, she is a sweet kid, really, but she just can't keep up with what we are doing in class."***

Practitioner: ***"Okay, how is she sweet?"*** **[starts with strengths]**

Mrs. Martinez: ***"Well, she has friends and is super polite with adults. She smiles a lot and seems pretty happy."***

Practitioner: ***"That's good. So, what do you mean when you say she can't keep up?"***

Mrs. Martinez: ***"Well, she was way behind in the last benchmark testing. She is supposed to be at Level 4 and she is barely at Level 2."*** **[test information]**

Practitioner: ***"How does that compare to the rest of your students?"*** **[class comparison]**

Mrs. Martinez: ***"I only have two other students at that level. One is an English learner who just moved here from the Middle East and the other is a boy in special education. So, she is a lot behind."***

Practitioner: ***"Is she falling further behind or did she just start behind and can't catch up?"*** **[rate of progress]**

Mrs. Martinez: ***"Well, she did start behind but I would say she is falling further behind, too. She just isn't learning as fast as most of the other students."***

Practitioner: ***"Alright, I understand. Is it mostly in reading or other subjects as well?"***

Mrs. Martinez: ***"She is a little behind in math but mostly reading. In writing, she has good ideas but doesn't spell very well. I am not too worried about that."***

Practitioner: ***"Okay, can we break down reading a bit? For example, how does she do in reading words versus reading comprehension?"*** *[***within-subject comparison***]*

Mrs. Martinez: ***"She seems to understand things if she can read them. Or, if I read something aloud to the class, she asks questions and seems to be on target but she hasn't caught on to phonics very well and reads really slowly. You can really tell if she reads aloud. She really labors sounding out the words and she doesn't seem to know many of them automatically. You know, by sight."***

Practitioner: ***"Okay, if I have this right, you think that if she could read something accurately and fast enough, she would understand it? And, her listening seems pretty good?"***

Mrs. Martinez: ***"Yes, that sounds about right."***

Practitioner: ***"Just to be sure, she attends and listens pretty well across different subjects?"***

Mrs. Martinez: ***"Yes, I would say so."***

Practitioner: ***"How well does she follow class routines and your directions ... say, when you change activities?"*** *[***switch from skills to classroom performance***]*

Mrs. Martinez: ***"Again, pretty well. She doesn't like to read aloud and doesn't like to be called on when we are reading something together as a class."***

Practitioner: ***"How about group work or working with other kids?"***

Mrs. Martinez: ***"She likes that a lot! She can be pretty chatty with her peers."***

Practitioner: ***"So, last question. What kinds of things have you tried so far to help?"*** *[***prior attempted solutions***]*

Mrs. Martinez: ***"I have tried to work with her a bit one on one but it's hard with such a big class. But, when I do that, she really likes it and I think she benefits."***

Practitioner: ***"Anything else? Maybe something you have been thinking about but haven't tried yet."***

Mrs. Martinez: ***"Well, we have this new program where the kids can come in early for about a half hour before school. I thought that would be good for her."***

Practitioner: ***"That seems like a good idea. Especially when she seems to do so well with you one on one. Could you get that going until the Multidisciplinary Team meets and we sort out what else we can do?"***

Mrs. Martinez: ***"Sure, I will talk with her mom tomorrow and see if she can come in early."***

Practitioner: ***"Great! Let me know how that goes or if you need me to talk with Mom, okay? I will get back to you if I think of any more questions. Otherwise, we will see each other at the meeting."***

Following this short interview, the school counselor knows that Mary has several strengths, including oral language, following classroom routines, and teacher directions. She also does well in math and seems to be well adjusted socially. At the same time, she struggles to keep up in reading and seems to have difficulties learning to read words fluently. This information, along with an interview with Mary, can play an important role in guiding further, more formal assessments and the development of appropriate strategies and interventions.

Chapter 9 Takeaway Points

- School-based practitioners are in a unique position to offer useful information to teachers and parents about the acquisition of academic skills or improving classroom behavior.
- Interviews of children about their experience doing academic work can help us understand their experiences and determine goals or how instruction might be changed.
- Interview topics include students' likes and dislikes at school, experiences doing homework, and relationships toward teachers. They also include whether students think they understand the assignment, feel confident about completing the assignment, or think they have enough time to complete it.
- Other strategies include academically focused *clinical interviews* and *curriculum-based assessment*.
- Teachers are critical informants in the assessment process, especially when the reason for the referral is academic achievement.
- Interviewing teachers makes use of many of the same basic strategies as interviewing students or parents.
- It is important to understand the impact of academic skill acquisition and the ability to perform in the classroom.
- Interviewing teachers about academic achievement often involves comparisons with external referents, for example, state or school district standards, other children in the class, what might be expected by someone of the same grade and background, and so on. It also involves within-person comparisons, for example, math versus reading, and so on.
- It is important to understand how students perform in the different aspects of an academic skill—for example, reading words versus comprehension or math computation versus applied math.

References

Anderson, H., & Goolishian, H. (1992). The client is the expert: A not-knowing approach to therapy. In S. McNamee & K. Gergen (Eds.), *Social construction and the therapeutic process* (pp. 25–39). Newbury Park, CA: Sage.

Clay, M. M. (2005). *Literacy lessons designed for individuals, part one: Why? When? and How?* Portsmouth, NH: Heinemann.

Deno, S. (1992). The nature and development of curriculum-based measurement. *Preventing School Failure, 36*(2), 5–10.

De Shazer, S. (1988). *Clues: investigating solutions in brief therapy*. New York, NY: W.W. Norton.

Fried, M. (Fall, 2013). Activating teaching: Using running records to inform teaching decisions. *Journal of Reading Recovery,* 5–16.

Ginsburg, H. (1981). The clinical interview in psychological research on mathematical thinking: Aims, rationales, techniques. *For the Learning of Mathematics, 1*(3), 4–11.

Ginsburg, H. P. (1997). *Entering the child's mind: The clinical interview in psychological research and practice*. New York, NY: Cambridge University Press.

Ginsburg, H. P., Lee, Y., & Pappas, S. (2016). Using the clinical interview and curriculum based measurement to examine risk levels. *Zdm, 48(7)*, 1031–1048. doi:10.1007/s11858-016-0802-z

Lipp, J. R., & Helfrich, S. R. (2016). Key reading recovery strategies to support classroom guided reading instruction. *Reading Teacher, 69*(6), 639–646.

McConaughy, S. H. (2013). *Clinical interviews for children and adolescents: Assessment to intervention*. New York, NY: Guilford Press.

Shapiro, E. S. (2011). *Academic skills problems: Direct assessment and intervention*. New York, NY: Guilford Press.

Shinn, M. R. (2002). Best practices in using curriculum-based measurement in a problem-solving model. In A. Thomas & J. Grimes (Eds.), *Best practices in school psychology IV* (pp. 671–697). Bethesda, MD: National Association of School Psychologists.

CHAPTER 10

Interviewing to Understand Strengths and Resources

This chapter is the mirror image of the chapter on clarifying and labeling problems. Using many of the same interviewing strategies we have discussed in other chapters, the goal is to name and clarify the strengths and resources clients draw upon to live their lives. Including an assessment of strengths is important for several reasons. One is that when students' strengths are recognized and named by adult practitioners, students feel more empowered and are more likely to actively take part in the assessment process and later treatment (Epstein, Hertzog, & Reid, 2001; Murphy, 2013; Nickerson & Fishman, 2013). Gathering information about strengths also broadens the focus of assessment to include building competence and enhancing skills rather than simply trying to reduce symptoms or problem behaviors (Epstein et al., 2001; Nickerson, 2007). Reducing the negative impact of problems is, of course, important but evidence suggests that the presence of various forms of personal and social competence in children is a more accurate predictor of better functioning later in adulthood than simply the absence of emotional and behavioral symptoms (Kohlberg, Ricks, & Snarey, 1972, 1984).

There are several influences on the impetus to include strengths as part of an assessment. One, of course, is positive psychology (Seligman, 2004), which has increasingly become of interest to school-based practitioners (Furlong, Gilman, & Huebner, 2014; Murphy, 2013). Using positive psychology as a framework, practitioners and researchers have developed a variety of assessments and interventions that focus on increasing well-being or happiness by promoting the experience of positive emotions (Fredrickson, 2001) or qualities such as gratitude (Emmons & Stern, 2013), hope (Pedrotti, Edwards, & Lopez, 2008), or optimism (Gillham, Reivich, & Shatté, 2001).

A second important influence is the study of resilience (Masten, 2014). Research on resilience grew out of research with children whose parents had serious mental illnesses (Luthar, Cicchetti, & Becker, 2000). The finding that many children of mentally ill parents seemed to do well in life despite the adversities they faced led researchers to an interest in a set of social and psychological factors that seemed to promote positive outcomes among children who faced adversities such as poverty, physical abuse, and sexual abuse (e.g., Garmezy, 1993; Masten & Curtis, 2000; Rutter, 2013). Researchers found that although it was true that children exposed to these stresses often have more psychosocial problems than those who were not exposed, the large majority still grew up to lead productive adult lives (e.g., Benard, 2004; Cicchetti, Rogosch, Lynch, & Holt, 1993; Werner & Smith, 2001).

Masten (2014) has argued there are basic psychosocial systems that, when functioning well, are universally protective of human development and form the core of resilience. These adaptive systems include (a) attachment and close relationships; (b) intelligence, ingenuity, and problem solving; (c) self-regulation and self-direction; (d) mastery motivation and sense of personal agency; and (e) faith, hope and belief that life has meaning (pp. 147–164). Using similar language, Benard (2004) proposes two broad categories of resilience: personal or phenomenological strengths and environmental protective factors. Personal strengths include (a) social competence, (b) problem solving, (c) autonomy, and (d) sense of purpose. Environmental protective factors can be found in families, communities, or schools and include (a) caring relationships; (b) clear and positive achievement expectations by family members, educators, and community members; and (c) opportunities to take part, contribute, and give back (Benard, 2004).

If strengths are to be taken seriously in assessment, they must be systematically recognized and named. Although we do not have a *DSM* or the parallel to IDEA's list of 13 disabilities, positive psychology and research on resilience offer a road map for what to look for when interviewing for strengths. These can be summarized as:

- The quality of relationships with peers and family
- The presence of cognitive or academic competencies, including skills used outside the classroom
- The presence of aspirations, goals, and plans
- The sense that despite adversity, there is a purpose to life
- A sense of agency or confidence in the ability to affect life and meet one's goals

In the following section, I will discuss specific questions and strategies to explore the contours of clients' strengths.

Tools for Eliciting Strengths

Although not a tool per se, the first step for practitioners interested in incorporating strengths into their assessments is to adopt the assumption that every child, family, or community has resources and capacities (Saleebey, 2008). We listen for and pay attention to what we believe is salient in an assessment. If we assume that strengths are always present, even if our clients are not aware of them, we become more curious about them and ask questions that add detail and increase our understanding of how these strengths contribute to their lives and how they can be used to better their situations.

What tools do we then apply to unpack strengths once we have developed a greater interest in them? Saleebey (2008) discusses eight kinds of questions that help further the discussion of strengths: (1) perspective questions, (2) change questions, (3) meaning questions, (4) survival questions, (5) support questions, (6) possibility questions, (7) exception questions, and (8) esteem questions (p. 73). Next, I elaborate on these questions and show how they might look in a dialogue with 16-year-old John, who is a junior in high school and lives in a local group home for foster youth.

Perspective Questions

Beginning with Chapter 1, I have argued for the importance of the insider perspective in assessment. With what Saleebey (2008) calls perspective questions, we return to this theme. As I have noted in prior chapters, the insider or emic perspective offers ecological validity for information from other sources and facilitates the working relationship needed to gather information during an assessment and successfully develop interventions. When we are curious about children's perspectives, we also encourage autonomy and competence by signaling that what they themselves think or feel about their situations is important. These questions set the stage for a discussion of strengths. Examples include:

- "What do you think is going on? What makes you think that?"
- "What are your ideas about how you got to this point with your school work?"
- "What have you been successful at so far?"
- "How do you explain your successes to yourself?"
- "How did you make that happen?"

Change Questions

Change questions are an extension of perspective questions. As part of the strengths perspective, we also assume that our clients, no matter how young or disturbed, are always trying to solve their problems even if they have been unsuccessful so far. Embedded in these efforts is our clients' theory of change (Duncan & Miller, 2000). Given the assumption that clients have been working on their problems in some way long before we interview them, it leads us to be curious about what they have done so far and, more importantly, what they have done that worked, if only partially (De Jong & Berg, 2013; Duncan & Miller, 2000). These questions might include:

- "What have you or someone done to try to make things better? How have those things worked?"
- "What do you think might make things better?"
- "What would be helpful for us to do to make things better?"
- "Lots of time, kids have good ideas about how to solve a problem. What do you think would help?"

Meaning Questions

Meaning questions are an extension of perspective questions. They try to get at what values, beliefs, or aspirations clients find important to them. Some of these are, of course, cultural and involve values or beliefs that the person views as shared by members of that community. These might include respect for elders, expectations for gender roles, the role of education in success in life, and so on. Other beliefs arise from personal experiences or experiences in a family that create what cognitive behavioral therapists refer to as core beliefs (Creed, Reisweber & Beck, 2011). Creed et al. describe core beliefs as the foundation for how we see ourselves, relate to others, and experience the world. These values and beliefs can, of course, be helpful or, they can be limiting. In an investigation of strengths, the focus is on beliefs that seem to sustain the person and become a source of resilience. Meaning questions include:

- "What is the most important thing about school for you?"
- "What did your family or friends teach you about what is important in life?"
- "What do you think your purpose in life is?"
- "What parts of your life do you think are most important?"

Survival Questions

Survival questions have also been referred to as *coping questions* (De Jong & Berg, 2013). They refocus attention away from feeling overwhelmed or helpless in the face of problems and toward clients' ways of dealing with their circumstances. Survival questions offer a window into potential strengths and help interviewers assess what strengths have been drawn upon in the face of adversity—that is, resilience. It is important to understand that although these efforts at coping have not necessarily been 100 percent successful, they may have been helpful in small ways that can be built upon in developing plans and interventions.

Survival questions acknowledge that things have been difficult, even overwhelming, but also assume that no matter how challenging circumstances are, people are also trying to deal with their problems in some way, even if only to just passively accept or ignore them. These normalizing statements communicate that clients' thoughts and feelings are unsurprising given the circumstances they face.

The simplest way of starting a conversation about survival or coping is to ask, "What has helped so far?" (De Jong & Berg, 2013). Other questions include:

- "That sounds really tough. How have you managed to cope with all that?"
- "Wow, I am amazed you made it to school today. How did you do that?"
- "I am not surprised you feel overwhelmed. Given all that is going on, has anything helped, even if only a little bit?"

Support Questions

Often one of the ways in which clients cope is to access social support. The importance of social connections and support is one of the most consistent findings in research on resilience (e.g., Benard, 2004; Masten, 2014; Werner & Smith, 2001). Seeking social support begins early in development with attachment to a parent or caregiver and expands as children grow older to include adults and peers in schools, neighborhoods, and community institutions (Masten, 2014). One strategy for eliciting information about clients' social networks is the *ecomap* discussed in Chapter 4. Other interview questions include:

- "What are your friends like (ages, gender)? What are some things you like to do together?"
- "Who are you closest to in your family? How are you close?"
- "Who in your life helps you reach your goals or explore your interests?"
- "Name some people that you respect or that you see doing things you like or appreciate. What kinds of things do they do?"
- "Do you belong to any clubs, teams, community organizations, or churches (synagogues, temples, etc.)?"
- "What family, friends, professionals, institutions, organizations, etc., have supported you? How? Are they still around? Do they still help?"

Another aspect of social connectedness is the notion of *required helpfulness* (Rachman, 1979). In many families, children assume the responsibility for caring for younger siblings, elderly grandparents, or ill parents (Werner & Smith, 1992). These social responsibilities can build confidence and a sense of competence in children or adolescents that fosters the belief that they can be successful in the face of adversity. Interview questions that focus on required helpfulness include:

- "Who counts on you? What do you do for them?"
- "Tell me about a time you did something nice for someone else, or you helped them out. What types of things do you enjoy doing for others?"
- "How do you help out around the house?"

Possibility Questions

It is difficult to underestimate the power of dreams, aspirations, and goals. As the astrophysicist and philosopher Erich Jantsch put it, "Mental anticipation now pulls the future into the present and reverses the direction of causality" (1980, p. 14). All the children and adolescents we assess are facing adversity of one kind or another. It is important for school counselors and school psychologists to remember that the children and adolescents we work with can be pulled into the future by "mental anticipation" of a vision of themselves that goes beyond whatever their current difficulties are. Possibility questions clarify these dreams and aspirations, making them more vivid and possible. Possibility questions include the *miracle question* used by practitioners of solution-focused brief therapy (De Jong & Berg, 2013). Other possibility questions include:

- "So, if we could figure out a way to solve this problem, how would things be better?"
- "If things went well for you, where would you be in a year?"
- "What do want to get out of school?"
- "What do you dream about doing with your life?"

Exception Questions

Exceptions are experiences when a problem might have happened but did not (De Shazer, 1988). Like survival questions, exceptions are windows into potential strengths. Practitioners of solution-focused brief therapy (De Jong & Berg, 2013) use the acronym EARS to frame the process of interviewing for exceptions. *E* stands for *elicit*. Eliciting exceptions starts with learning to listen for and recognize exceptions. Exceptions can be found in school documents or records (Murphy, 2015), for example, evidence of past good grades, or of doing better in certain classes even when not doing well in others. Eliciting exceptions can also be as straightforward as simply asking, "Has there been a time recently when things were better for you?" Other exceptions-eliciting questions include:

- "When does it seem that Mrs. Jones is not on your back as much?"
- "When is this less of a problem?"
- "So, what things about school do you want to keep the way they are?"

The *A* in EARS stands for *amplify* (De Jong & Berg, 2013). Amplifying exceptions involves gathering details about how the exceptions happened and what role the client played in making them happen. Murphy (2015) points out that the details of exceptions should be pursued with the same energy that mental health practitioners use to gather details about clients' problems.

The *R* in EARS stands for *reinforce* (Murphy, 2015). Reinforcing exceptions can be simply celebrating successes, or what Kral and Kowalski (1989) call *cheerleading*. Cheerleading is a form of social reinforcement and can consist of simple statements such as:

- "Way to go!"
- "That's great!"
- "Wow! That's fantastic!"

Another aspect of reinforcing exceptions that can be combined with cheerleading is *positive blaming* (Kral & Kowalski, 1989) or *giving credit* (Murphy, 2015). Clients do not necessarily assume responsibility for what goes well and will often assume that when an exception takes place it is a lucky accident and not the result of their own actions. Positive blaming extends social reinforcement and helps clients make connections between their thoughts and behaviors, and exceptions. For example, if a client shares an exception, follow-up questions might be:

- "Great, how did you figure out such a good idea?"
- "That's great. So, what did you do to make it easier for that to happen?"
- "That is great that you were able to do that. What does it say about you that you were able to come up with such a good idea?"

Esteem Questions

Esteem questions are questions that investigate what someone does well, appreciates about themselves, or feels competent doing. They can be as straightforward as:

- "Which classes do you like best?"
- "What do you like to do in your free time?"

- "When do you feel really good about yourself?"
- "What do you enjoy most?"

Another type of question that can be helpful in exploring what someone does well is relationship questions. As discussed in Chapters 4 and 6, relationship questions allow the interviewer to access how clients think other people think about them. It also allows clients to name strengths or preferred activities without the social pressure of owning that quality or activity directly. Examples include:

- "What do people like about you?"
- "What would your friends say you were good at?"
- "So, if your dad were here, what would he say that you did well around the house?"

A Conversation About Strengths

An assessment is a process of trying to understand what works and does not work in the lives of the clients we work with (Lopez, Snyder, & Rasmussen, 2003). To arrive at the balanced and holistic view that this statement suggests, the goal is give strengths "equal space, equal time, equal emphasis" (Lopez et al., 2003, p. 17) with problems. Conceptually, this is straightforward. In practice, this can be more difficult. The following conversation between a school psychologist and John, a 16-year-old junior in high school who lives at a local group home for foster youth, illustrates how the questions we have just discussed may look in an actual interview. John's teachers referred him for an assessment because recently he is finishing less of his work and he seems more withdrawn. Currently, John receives special education services under the IDEIA category of *other health impairment* because of a diagnosis of ADHD.

Practitioner: ***"Hello John, I think you have seen me around school. You know I am the school psychologist, right?"***

John: ***"Yeah, you came to my health class once to talk about suicide."***

Practitioner: ***"Yeah, that was me. Your teachers said they are worried about how things are going for you. They said it seems like you aren't doing as much work as you did and are a bit more withdrawn."***

John: ***"I don't know, maybe ... I guess I'm not doing as much work."***

Practitioner: ***"Well, before we get on to that can I ask you some other questions?"***

John: ***"Sure, go ahead."***

Practitioner: ***"Okay, to start, what classes do you like best?"*** **[esteem question]**

John: ***"I guess math and social studies."***

Practitioner: ***"Okay, what do you like about them?"***

John: ***"I am pretty good at math, and I like the story part of social studies. You know … learning about how people lived and stuff."***

Practitioner: ***"Great, so, you do pretty well in those classes then?"***

John: ***"Yeah, I am still doing okay in those classes. Better than the others."***

Practitioner: ***"How about your free time. What do you enjoy doing then?" [*****esteem question*****]***

John: ***"I like to play the guitar and watch TV. I would play video games but they won't let us play them at the house."***

Practitioner: ***"So, what is the most important thing about school for you?" [*****meaning question*****]***

John: ***"I know I got to go to college to get a good job. I don't want to end up like my dad. He's in jail, you know."***

Practitioner: ***"No, I didn't know that. So, getting a good job is important to you and you think that going to college is the best way to day that. What kind of a good job do you think you might want?"***

John: ***"I don't know for sure but maybe something in tech; I like to fix things and figure out how stuff goes together."***

Practitioner: ***"That's great. Back to the thing with your teachers; what do you think is going on?" [*****perspective question*****]***

John: ***"I don't know … I just don't feel it anymore. Like I just want to space out and do nothing."***

Practitioner: ***"Oh, okay. What do you think that is about?"***

John: ***"Not sure … there is so much going on. At the group home, they keep talking about how I need to get ready for when I graduate but that scares the crap out of me. They suck!"***

Practitioner: ***"I am not surprised you feel scared. Given all that is going on … has anything helped, even if only a little bit?" [*****normalizing statement and survival question*****]***

John: ***[frowns and looks down] "My history teacher is nice. She wasn't in a home but she said she had to leave her house because her dad was a nut case. It is cool to listen to her talk about stuff like that."***

Practitioner: ***[smiles and nods] "Sounds like she is a great support for you. Who else can you count on?" [*****support question*****]***

John: ***"I like my therapist at the home … she is pretty easy to talk with."***

Practitioner: ***"That's good … I wonder what do you think might make things better for you?" [*****change question*****]***

John: ***"Don't know … get more work done."***

Practitioner: ***"Okay, so if things went well for you and you were able to do that, where would you be in a year?"*** **[possibility question]**

John: ***"I would be about to graduate ... that's crazy ... maybe I would have a college picked out."***

Practitioner: ***"Great, John. So, let me see if get this all straight. You are pretty good at math and social studies. You like to play the guitar and you are pretty close to your history teacher. Also, you want to go to college and for sure don't want to end up like your dad. I just want to say that you have a lot going for you.*** **[summary of strengths and amplification]** ***Going back to not being motivated and getting enough, what was different when that was better?"*** **[elicit exception question]**

John: ***"I guess I wasn't thinking so much about what happens after school. It freaks me out."***

Practitioner: ***"What do think would help not think about it so much? I guess you could distract yourself or sometimes I heard that when you make a plan about something it leads you not to worry so much."***

John: ***"A plan ... just thinking about it makes me feel weird."***

Practitioner: ***"I wonder if you might start by talking to your history teacher. She must have done something when she left home."***

John: ***"Yeah, I am okay talking with her."***

Practitioner: ***"That is great. Before we stop, I have one more question. On a scale of 1 to 10—10 is you are totally freaked out and 1 is you are completely calm—where are you today?"***

John: ***"I was an 8 when we started but maybe a 6 now."***

Practitioner: ***"Okay, that's fantastic. So, let's see where you are after talking to your history teacher. Let's talk in a couple of days, okay?"***

John: ***"Sure."***

Reading this dialogue, it is important to notice that the practitioner spent little time in this short session exploring John's symptoms. Given what John shared, the practitioner would, of course, be remiss to not take note that his loss of motivation in the face of an overwhelming future could be a sign of depression. It would also be important to note that John's ADHD may make it more difficult to make a systematic plan. These things are important, but it is equally important to know that John has aspirations, goals, hobbies, and connections with other adults. A balanced approach to assessment takes the whole person, including resources, strengths, and barriers to success into consideration.

Chapter 10 Takeaway Points

- Including an assessment of strengths is important because when students' strengths are recognized and named by adult practitioners, students feel more empowered and are more likely to actively take part in the assessment process and later treatment.
- A model of strengths can be derived from positive psychology and research on resilience. A simple model would include:
  - The quality of relationships with peers and family
  - The presence of cognitive or academic competencies, including skills used outside the classroom
  - The presence of aspirations, goals, and plans
  - The sense that despite adversity, there is a purpose to life
  - A sense of confidence or ability to affect life to meet one's goals
- Assessing strengths requires a shift in perspective to assuming the presence of strengths, even when they are hard to see.
- Saleebey (2008) discusses eight kinds of questions that help further discussion of strengths: (1) perspective questions, (2) change questions, (3) meaning questions, (4) survival questions, (5) support questions, (6) possibility questions, (7) exception questions, and (8) esteem questions.
- We should strive to give strengths "equal space, equal time, equal emphasis" (Lopez et al., 2003, p. 17).

References

Benard, B. (2004). *Resiliency: What we have learned*. San Francisco, CA: WestEd.

Cicchetti, D., Rogosch, F. A., Lynch, M., & Holt, K. D. (1993). Resilience in maltreated children: Processes leading to adaptive outcome. *Development & Psychopathology, 5*(4), 629–647. doi:10.1017/S0954579400006209

Creed, T. A., Reisweber, J., & Beck, A. T. (2011). *Cognitive therapy for adolescents in school settings*. New York, NY: Guilford Press.

De Jong, P., & Berg, I. K. (2013). *Interviewing for solutions*. Belmont, CA: Brooks/Cole, Cengage Learning.

De Shazer, S. (1988). *Clues: investigating solutions in brief therapy*. New York, NY: W.W. Norton. doi:10.1177/0533316412474924

Duncan, B. L., & Miller, S. D. (2000). The client's theory of change: Consulting the client in the integrative process. *Journal of Psychotherapy Integration, 10*(2), 169–187. doi:10.1023/A:1009448200244

Emmons, R. A., & Stern, R. (2013). Gratitude as a psychotherapeutic intervention. *Journal of Clinical Psychology, 69*(8), 846–855. doi:10.1002/jclp.22020

Epstein, M. H., Hertzog, M. A., & Reid, R. (2001). The Behavioral and Emotional Rating Scale: Long term test–retest reliability. *Behavioral Disorders, 26*(4), 314–320.

Fredrickson, B. L. (2001). The role of positive emotions in positive psychology: The broaden-and-build theory of positive emotions. *The American Psychologist, 56*(3), 218–226.

Furlong, M. J., Gilman, R., & Huebner, E. S. (2014). *Handbook of positive psychology in schools* (2nd ed.). New York, NY: Routledge.

Garmezy, N. (1993). Children in poverty: Resilience despite risk. *Psychiatry, 56,* 127–136.

Gillham, J. E., Reivich, K. J., & Shatté, A. J. (2001). Building optimism and preventing depressive symptoms in children. In E. C. Chang (Ed.), *Optimism and pessimism: Implications for theory, research, and practice* (pp. 301–320). Washington, DC, US: American Psychological Association. doi:10.1037/10385-014

Jantsch, E. (1980). *The self-organizing universe: Scientific and human implications of the emerging paradigm of evolution*. Oxford, England: Pergamon Press.

Kohlberg, L., & Ricks, D., & Snarey, J. (1972). The predictability of adult mental health from childhood behavior. In B. B. Wolman (Ed.), *Manual of child psychopathology* (pp. 1217–1284). New York, NY: McGraw-Hill.

Kohlberg, L., & Ricks, D., & Snarey, J. (1984). Childhood development as a predictor of adaptation in adulthood. *Genetic Psychology Monographs, 110,* 91–172.

Kral, R., & Kowalski, K. (1989). After the miracle: The second stage in solution focused brief therapy. *Journal of Strategic & Systemic Therapies, 8*(2–3), 73–76.

Lopez, S. J., Snyder, C. R., & Rasmussen, H. N. (2003). Striking a vital balance: Developing a complementary focus on human weakness and strength through positive psychological assessment. In S. J. Lopez & C. R. Snyder (Eds.), *Positive psychological assessment: A handbook of models and measures* (pp. 3–20). Washington, DC: American Psychological Association.

Luthar, S. S., Cicchetti, D., & Becker, B. (2000). The construct of resilience: A critical evaluation and guidelines for future work. *Child Development, 71*(3), 543–562.

Masten, A. S. (2014). *Ordinary magic: Resilience in development*. New York, NY: Guilford Press.

Masten, A. S., & Curtis, W. J. (2000). Integrating competence and psychopathology: Pathways toward a comprehensive science of adaption in development. *Development and Psychopathology, 12*(3), 529–550. doi:10.1017/S095457940000314X

Murphy, J. J. (2013). Student-driven interviewing: Practical strategies for building strength-based interventions. *Communique, 41*(7), 1.

Murphy, J. J. (2015). *Solution-focused counseling in schools* (3rd ed.). Alexandria, VA: American Counseling Association.

Nickerson, A. B. (2007). The use and importance of strength-based assessment. *School Psychology Forum: Research in Practice, 2,* 15–25.

Nickerson, A. B., & Fishman, C. E. (2013). Promoting mental health and resilience through strength-based assessment in US schools. *Educational and Child Psychology, 30*(4), 7–17.

References

Pedrotti, J. T., Edwards, L. M., & Lopez, S. J. (2008). Promoting hope: Suggestions for school counselors. *Professional School Counseling, 12*(2), 100–107.

Rachman, S. (1979). The concept of required helpfulness. *Behaviour Research and Therapy, 17*(1), 1–6. doi:10.1016/0005-7967(79)90044-5

Rutter, M. (2013). Annual research review: Resilience—Clinical implications. *Journal of Child Psychology and Psychiatry, 54*(4), 474–487. doi:10.1111/j.1469-7610.2012.02615.x

Saleebey, D. (2008). Commentary on the strengths perspective and potential applications in school counseling. *Professional School Counseling, 12*(2), 68–75.

Seligman, M. P. (2004). *Authentic happiness: Using the new positive psychology to realize your potential for lasting fulfillment*. New York, NY: Free Press.

Werner, E. E., & Smith, R. S. (1992). *Overcoming the odds: High risk children from birth to adulthood*. Ithaca, NY: Cornell University Press.

Werner, E. E., & Smith, R. S. (2001). *Journeys from childhood to midlife: Risk, resilience, and recovery*. Ithaca, NY: Cornell University Press.

CHAPTER 11

Interviewing in High-Risk Situations: Suicide Assessment

This chapter will focus on interviewing when there is a risk of suicide. Interviewing when clients are distressed enough to think of harming themselves is uniquely challenging and, as Sommers-Flanagan and Sommers-Flanagan put it, "having responsibility for someone else's lethal impulses is both frightening and stressful" (2012, p. 246). The goal of this chapter is to provide interview guidelines that will allow practitioners to assess the threat posed by students' thoughts, feelings, and behaviors and to develop a plan to increase safety.

Both internationally and in the United States, suicide is one of the leading causes of death among adolescents. The World Health Organization estimates that suicide accounts for 100,000 adolescent deaths and 4 million attempts annually (Fleischmann et al., 2008), making it the second leading cause of death for older adolescents globally (World Health Organization [WHO], 2014). In the United States, suicide is the second leading cause of death among school-aged children and youth (Centers for Disease Control and Prevention [CDC], 2016b).

According to 2015 data from the Youth Risk Behavior survey (Kann et al., 2016), 17.7% of adolescents in the United States reported seriously considering suicide, 14.6% reported making a plan to kill themselves, and 8.6% had attempted suicide one or more times. Data such as this can sometimes feel abstract, but concretely this means that a school counselor or school psychologist who works at a high school with 2,000 students could potentially deal with 354 students who are considering suicide, 292 students who have made a plan to kill themselves, and 172 students who attempt suicide.

This risk is not evenly distributed in the population of adolescents. For example, males are almost twice as likely to die from suicide even though females are nearly twice as likely to think about killing themselves or to make plans to end their lives (CDC, 2016a). Sexual minority youth are also at much higher risk of suicide than their heterosexual and cissexual peers (Marshal et al., 2011).

Theories of how suicide develops can be helpful in understanding what to focus on during an assessment interview. For example, Shneidman (1993) argued that unbearable *psychache,* or psychological pain, is an essential condition for suicide to occur. Shneidman defined psychache as the "hurt, anguish, soreness, aching, psychological pain in the psyche, the mind" (p. 145). For persons to consider suicide as a viable option they must view their psychological pain as unbearable and see death as the only possible solution.

More recently, researchers who study suicide have begun to focus on ideation-to-action theories of suicide that seek to understand the movement from thinking of suicide to attempting suicide (Miller, 2018). The interpersonal theory of suicide (ITS; Joiner, 2005; Van Orden et al., 2010) proposes that people die by suicide after developing two qualities: (1) a passive desire to die and (2) an increased capability to kill themselves. The desire to die arises from a combination of *thwarted belongingness* and *perceived burdensomeness*. Thwarted belongingness occurs when people desire to connect with others but perceive themselves as unable to do this, resulting in a feeling of social isolation. When this joins with the perception that one's life is a burden to others, the result is a desire to die.

Per ITS, a desire to die is passive in that by itself it is not a sufficient condition for suicidal behavior. In addition to the desire to die, those who attempt suicide must also develop the capacity to take action on this desire, which comes from a *lowered fear of death* and *elevated pain tolerance* (Joiner, 2005; Van Orden et al., 2010). Fear of death has been shown to be a protective factor among those who express the desire to die (Linehan, Goodstein, Nielsen, & Chiles, 1983). Conversely, if clients are to move from a passive desire to die to taking steps to make that happen, the thought of dying must become less frightening. In addition, it is also necessary to reduce the fear of pain to the point where the potential pain involved in the method one has chosen seems tolerable (Joiner, 2005; Van Orden et al., 2010). ITS provides a way to understand interviewing to assess risk.

INTERVIEWING TO ASSESS RISK

Suicide risk assessment has been conceptualized as a three-part process: (1) gathering information about risk and protective factors; (2) gathering information about warning signs such as suicidal ideation, intentions, plans, and behaviors; and (3) using these two different sources of information to estimate risk (Shea, 2009). Warning signs are immediate signs or symptoms that indicate the desire to die and/or an increased capacity to take action on that desire. Risk factors are less immediate and are characteristics of persons, families, or their broader family, social, or historical factors that research has shown to increase a person's vulnerability to attempting suicide. Risk increases when warning signs interact with risk factors. For example, a person who expresses thoughts of killing himself (warning sign indicating a passive desire to die) but also indicates he has thought of a particular means of carrying out that desire (warning sign indicating potential increased capability) is certainly at risk for killing himself, but if this person is also depressed and has made prior attempts, that risk increases significantly.

The primary difference between warning signs and risk factors is that warning signs are proximal, whereas risk factors can have a distal relationship to suicide. In other words, risk factors are background, whereas warning signs are related to immediate functioning. As Rudd puts it:

> Warning signs help to answer the critical question: What is my patient doing (observable signs) or saying (expressed symptoms, that elevates his or her risk to die by suicide in the next few minutes, hours or days? (2008, p. 87)

Suicide assessments should focus on both of these broad factors, but warning signs should carry more weight in the decisions that take place in the short term following an assessment because they are often indications of a suicide crisis that represents immediate risk.

Warning Signs

Using ITS as a framework, warning signs consist of signs (observable behaviors) and symptoms (what is expressed by the person but not necessarily directly observable) that are expressions of an increased desire to die and a growing capacity to act on this desire (Joiner, 2005; Van Orden et al., 2010). The expert consensus panel of the American Association of Suicidology has agreed that (a) talking or writing about death, dying, or suicide; (b) threatening to kill oneself; (c) looking for ways to kill oneself; and (d) seeking access to means are signs of acute risk that call for immediate attention (American Association of Suicidology, n.d.). The first warning sign—talking or writing about death, dying, or suicide—represents ideation or an increased passive desire to die. Actual threats to kill oneself represent an escalation in the desire to die but also might indicate the likelihood of a growing capacity to kill oneself. The last warning sign listed earlier—seeking access to means—suggests the person has moved from a passive desire to die to an increased capacity to kill oneself and suggests acute danger.

Risk Factors

Risk factors are characteristics of persons, their histories, or the environments people live in, that have been shown to have an empirical relationship with increased suicidality

(Rudd et al., 2006). They do not have the same temporal relationship to suicide as warning signs, and do not necessarily indicate immediate risk. Warning signs indicate a suicide crisis and acute immediate risk, whereas risk factors suggest risk over much longer periods of time, ranging from a year to a lifetime (Rudd, Joiner, & Rajab, 2001). It is also important to note that although research has shown a strong relationship between risk factors and suicide ideation – passive desire to die in the ITS model – they poorly predict suicide attempts (Klonsky, Qiu, & Saffer; 2017).

As discussed earlier, an important risk factor in suicide is mental illness. Other important risk factors are prior attempts and substance or alcohol abuse. One study found that about two-thirds of a sample of 120 completed suicides had one of these three risk factors: (1) prior attempts, (2) depressive disorder, and (3) substance abuse and alcohol disorder (Shaffer et al., 1996). As discussed earlier, the Youth Risk Behavior survey (Kann et al., 2016) found that in 2015, 8.6% of youth surveyed had made a prior suicide attempt one or more times. A much larger percentage of respondents, 29.9%, reported feeling so sad or hopeless almost every day for two or more weeks in a row that they had ceased doing at least some usual activities. Substance use varied, but 17.7% of students surveyed reported that they had drunk five or more drinks in a row in the 30 days before they had taken the survey. Nearly 22% had smoked marijuana and over 5% had used cocaine. It is important to understand that risk factors build upon one another and that co-occurrence is common (Shaffer et al., 1996).

In addition to prior attempts, depression, and substance abuse, impulsivity is also thought to be a significant risk factor for suicide (Kleiman, Riskind, Schaefer, & Weingarden, 2012). Impulsivity has been conceptualized as having four components: (1) urgency, (2) lack of perseverance, (3) lack of premeditation, and (4) sensation-seeking (Whiteside & Lynam, 2001). A study using this model of impulsivity found that elevated urgency, or the tendency to give in to strong impulses when experiencing strong negative emotions, distinguished both those who thought of suicide and those who made attempts from those who had never been suicidal (Klonsky & May, 2010). Another aspect of the model, lack of premeditation or the inability to think through the consequences of one's behavior, was found to distinguish those who had attempted suicide from both those who had thought of suicide and those who had never been suicidal (Klonsky & May, 2010). These results suggest that the relationship between impulsivity and suicide is complex, and practitioners should focus on particular aspects of the model to gain an accurate picture of risk.

Perhaps the most powerful protective factor for suicide is social support, which stands as the inverse to social isolation and feelings of burdensomeness discussed in ITS (Van Orden et al., 2010; Joiner, 2005). The importance of social support as a buffer to feelings of suicide goes back at least to Durkheim's (1951) theory that people who were not integrated socially with persons who shared common values and meanings were more likely to complete suicide. In contrast, social solidarity, or the extent to which persons were integrated into meaningful social networks, was a powerful protective factor. Social support has been identified as a buffer against the major risk factors associated with suicidality, including depression (Skärsäter, Langius, Ågren, Häggström, & Dencker, 2005; Underwood, 2000; WHO, 2001), substance abuse (Acri, Gogel, Pollock, & Wisdom, 2012; Richter, Brown, & Mott, 1991), and impulsivity (Kleiman et al., 2012). Including a brief assessment of social support as well as important risk factors is critical for a comprehensive assessment of suicide risk. It is important to note that interviewing clients about social support will provide information about their perceptions of social support rather than an objective measure of social support. When interviewing someone who is thinking of suicide, perceptions of social support are in many ways more important than actual social support. At the same time, social support that is perhaps not recognized by the client serves as a critical resource when developing interventions.

In the following dialogue, a school counselor interviews Paul, a 15-year-old boy who was referred by his teacher because of Paul's response to a writing assignment where he wrote things suggesting that he wanted to die and felt hopeless:

Practitioner: ***"Hello Paul, Mrs. Jimenez asked me to talk with you after she read what you wrote for your assignment."***

Paul: ***"Yeah, okay, I know what she is talking about."***

Practitioner: ***"Okay, good. She told me you wrote that life wasn't worth living and you wished you were dead. Would you mind telling me about your assignment and what led you to write about that?" [*Paul's writing suggests a passive desire to die.*]***

Paul: ***"I guess ... I don't know. The assignment was to write about the future and what you looked forward to but I don't really look forward to anything and think it is ... don't know ... like it all is a dead end."***

Practitioner: ***"You mean life? Life is a dead end?"***

Paul: ***"Yes ... I can't see the point. Bad shit happens and then you die anyway."***

Practitioner: ***"So, there is nothing to look forward to or nothing that you enjoy and think is worth sticking around for?" [*This is both a paraphrase but also a prompt for reasons to live.*]***

Paul: ***"Not really."***

Practitioner: ***"So Paul, I need to ask you some questions. The first one is: Are you or have you been thinking of killing yourself?" [*Paul has hinted at suicidality. This question attempts to gather more explicit information.*]***

Paul: ***"Yeah, I do sometimes."***

Practitioner: ***"Okay, how often would you say you have those thoughts?"***

Paul: ***"I have thought of it off and on for a while but lately, a lot ... every day really."***

Practitioner: ***"How far have you gotten with that—for example, have you thought of how you might do it?"***

Paul: ***"Sort of ... I don't want to shoot myself. That would just be too terrible for the person who found me but maybe I could take pills."***

Practitioner: ***"What kind of pills are you thinking about?"***

Paul: ***"I am not sure ... I don't know. My mom takes these pills to help her sleep. I am pretty sure that would do it."***

Practitioner: ***"Okay Paul, do you know where those pills are? [*****access to means*****]***

Paul: ***"She keeps them in her medicine cabinet in her bedroom."***

Practitioner: ***"Paul, I am going to switch gears here a bit. So, what is going on that you want to kill yourself?" [*****At this point the practitioner has gathered information about warning signs: threats to kill self, plans and access to means. The conversation will switch to risk factors.*****]***

Paul: ***"Like I said, I just don't see the point ... it just seems like nothing is going to work out and nothing seems worth doing anymore."***

Practitioner: ***"Anymore ... did things used to seem better?"***

Paul: ***"I guess ... things just went downhill when I switched schools last year. I don't see my friends and school is not going well."***

Practitioner: ***"So Paul, it sounds like this has been a super tough time. On a scale of 1 to 10, with 10 being the most depressed and hopeless and 1 being hardly at all, what number would you give yourself now?" [*****This scaling question gives the practitioner some idea of the extent of Paul's depression—a significant risk factor. It is important to note that a scaling question is self-anchored in that it assess perceptions.*****]***

Paul: ***"Maybe a 9 I guess. I am pretty bummed."***

Practitioner: ***"Okay, sounds like this transition to a new school has been really bad for you. Paul, I have to ask this but do you drink or use drugs, especially lately?" [*****risk factor—substance abuse*****]***

Paul: ***"No, I don't really drink ... once in a while I guess ... and I don't use drugs."***

Practitioner: ***"Have you ever thought about killing yourself before ... ever tried?" [*****risk factor of prior attempts*****]***

Paul: ***"No, up until pretty recently, things have been okay I guess. They are just shitty now."***

Practitioner: ***"Paul, if I asked one of your friends to describe you, what would they say? For example, are you shy or outgoing, or do you think about things for a long time or do you just do whatever comes to your mind, like you just go for it ... you know, that kind of stuff."***

Paul: ***"I think my friends see me as a little shy ... I don't know ... I guess I have to think about things for a while before I make up my mind about stuff."***

Practitioner: ***"Okay ... I have to ask. Has that been true for this? Have you thought about killing yourself for a long time?"***
Paul: ***"Yeah ... for a while."***
Practitioner: ***"Does anyone know about how you feel or your plans?"***
Practitioner: ***"My friend Anna knows a little about how I feel but I haven't said anything about thinking about killing myself."***

The information we have gathered about Paul is summarized next.

Warning signs

- Thinking of killing himself
- Some thought of a plan
- Has access to means

Risk factors

- Has undergone a significant life transition and appears depressed
- No indication of substance abuse and no history of prior attempts
- Does not appear to be impulsive

Paul is at significant risk because of the warning signs and his apparent depression. The good news is that he does not appear to abuse substances or be especially impulsive. We will return to Paul later after discussing interviewing to assure safety.

Interviewing to Assure Safety

As discussed in Chapter 1, all assessments should lead to interventions. In the case of the threat of suicide, at least one intervention may be notification of parents or even contacting emergency personnel to initiate hospitalization. This "assess and refer" model (Stanley & Brown, 2012) has limitations in that parents may not follow up on recommendations and students may return to school the next day without any change in their status. In addition, even if students are hospitalized or otherwise receive community-based treatment, they will typically need school-based support when they return to school.

In the short term, school-based practitioners can offer a brief intervention concurrently with a suicide risk assessment. The safety planning intervention (SPI; Stanley & Brown, 2012) has been proposed as a brief treatment for suicide in hospital emergency departments, trauma centers, in-patient psychiatric units, and suicide hotlines. Although the conditions that make a suicide can persist over time, a suicide crisis is often relatively short, and brief interventions such as SPI can be useful in that they can assist the person to cope with the crisis until suicidal thoughts lessen or other interventions can be implemented (Stanley & Brown, 2012).

SPI is different than no-harm contracts, which are agreements between a suicidal client and a practitioner that the client will not harm him- or herself. Although practitioners commonly use no-harm contracts, they lack a consistent format and strong empirical support for their efficacy (Edwards & Sachmann, 2010; Hansen et al., 2012). SPI instead focuses on specific forms of coping and is similar to other cognitive and behavioral interventions such as coping plans, *road map to success*, or *Hope Kit* (Creed, Reisweber, & Beck, 2011).

The components of an SPI include (a) recognition of personal warning signs, (b) internal coping strategies, (c) socialization strategies for distraction and support, (d) social contacts for assistance in resolving suicidal crisis, (e) professional contacts for assistance in resolving suicidal crisis, and (f) means restriction (Stanley & Brown, 2012). Personal warning signs are those thoughts, emotions, or behaviors that are antecedents to the suicide crisis. More concrete and specific descriptions of warning signs are more helpful to the client (Stanley & Brown, 2012). Internal coping strategies are ways that clients can distract themselves from the intense feelings and urges associated with the suicidal crisis. These can include activities such as going for a walk, listening to one's favorite music, exercising, reading an enjoyable book, and so on. Socialization strategies include socializing with friends or family members in naturally occurring social settings (Stanley, Biggs, & Brown, 2014). These strategies are intended to serve as a kind of distraction from the suicidal thoughts and are not meant to be situations where clients discuss their thoughts or feelings about suicide. On the other hand, social contacts for assistance in resolving the crisis involve clients explicitly revealing and discussing their thoughts and feelings about suicide. This could involve the same persons involved in distracting social activities, but care should be taken to make reasonably sure that the persons clients confide in will respond in a helpful and supportive manner (Stanley & Brown, 2012). Personal and agency contacts to help resolve suicidal crises are professionals, agencies, or hotlines that clients can contact if the prior strategies prove unsuccessful. Lastly, means restriction involves a plan that secures and makes less available the means that would allow clients to act on their suicidal impulses.

Next, we continue the dialogue with Paul with a focus on developing a safety plan:

Practitioner: ***"Okay Paul. As you can imagine, I am going to have to talk with your parents. When the time comes, we can talk over the best way to do that."***

Paul: ***"God, they are going to be super upset and pissed, especially my mom."***

Practitioner: ***"Like I said, we will discuss this more a bit later but for now, who would be the best person to discuss this with first?"***

Paul: ***"My dad. He'll be upset but he won't completely freak out."***

Practitioner: ***"Okay, we'll keep that in mind but if I can't get ahold of your dad, it will have to be your mom and, of course, she is going to find out anyway, right?"***

Paul: ***"Okay."***

Practitioner: ***"Paul, now I want to ask you some other kinds of questions and write the answers down on this form. I want to start with how did you first begin to notice that things were getting really bad … I mean, what did you feel? What did you do or stop doing and what did you think?"*** *[***personal warning signs***]*

Paul: ***"Not sure … I guess I stopped wanting to talk with other people and started spending a lot of time playing video games by myself. I just didn't have any energy … no life …. You know what I mean?"***

Practitioner: ***"So if I was to write here that you just didn't have any energy to do stuff, would that fit? What kinds of stuff didn't you feel you wanted to do?"***

Paul: ***"Like I said, hang out or talk with people. Even watching TV with my parents. I just felt like shit all the time."***

Practitioner: ***"Wow, that sounds like it really sucks. Like you were really hurting … I am going to write down not being around or communicating with people. Everyone does that a little. How long do you withdraw before you know it is a problem?"***

Paul: ***"A whole day, I guess. I live with my mom and dad so I should always talk with them at least a little."***

Practitioner: ***"Can you tell me a little more about what feeling like shit actually feels like?"***

Paul: ***"I just don't feel anything … like I am numb."***

Practitioner: ***"So I am going to write on this list feeling numb, okay? What are some things you might do that would kind of distract you from those feeling … positive things?"*** *[***internal coping strategies***]*

Paul: ***"Well, I used to play the guitar. I still have one in my room. I really like to play."***

Practitioner: ***"Cool, so one thing is play the guitar. What else?"***

Paul: ***"I know this sounds funny but I like to cook … you know just make stuff that I like to eat."***

Practitioner: ***"That is great. I don't think that is funny at all. I'll put that down too. How about at least one more thing."***

Paul: ***"Maybe watch TV."***

Practitioner: ***"You mean with someone in the living room, like that?"***

Paul: ***"Well, sometimes but even if no one is there, I like to watch some shows."***

Practitioner: ***"What about people you can hang out with when you start to feel numb. Not like to talk about it but just to hang out." [*socialization strategies*]***

Paul: ***"Well, the TV thing but my mom likes to watch this one show with me."***

Practitioner: ***"So, watching TV with you mom, who else?"***

Paul: ***"My friends Anna and Randy are cool. They know I have been down and like to do things to distract me."***

Practitioner: ***"Okay, your mom, Anna, and Randy. Anyone else?"***

Paul: ***"Maybe … I am not sure right now. Maybe that is all I guess."***

Practitioner: ***"Okay, I want to ask you about people again but about people that you could talk to about all this." [*social contacts that assist in resolving crisis*]***

Paul: ***"Not my mom for sure … maybe Anna. She is a good listener."***

Practitioner: ***"Okay, can you get ahold of Anna if you need to?"***

Paul: ***"Sure, she always answers texts and stuff really fast."***

Practitioner: ***"Okay, good. Now, you and I are going to think of some professionals you can contact if you need to, okay? I am going to write the number of a suicide hot line here for you. Do you work with a counselor or therapists outside of school?" [*professional resources to assist in resolving crisis*]***

Paul: ***"I did for a while but I haven't seen him for a while. I still have his number."***

Practitioner: ***"Okay, well, I will put his number here too but I am also going to put the number down of Metro Hospital. If things get really bad you can call them and they will help out for sure."***

Paul: ***"Okay."***

Practitioner: ***"Lastly, Paul, I am going to tell your mom and dad to put their medicines away somewhere where it is not easy to get to. I am going to write that down here too. I am going to make a copy of this form and give it to you, okay? Before your mom or dad come to get you, we'll go over it again. Now, let's talk about contacting your parents." [*means restriction*]***

Paul: ***"Okay, not looking forward to that."***

Practitioner: ***"I bet, but they need to know what is going on."***

Post–Suicide Attempt Interventions

Although this chapter concerns interviewing for assessment, what actions might follow a suicide attempt and the immediate response? The data on post suicide attempt interventions is sparse. The data that do exist suggests that *dialectical behavior therapy* (DBT; Linehan et al., 2006; Linehan et al., 2015) is effective in reducing both later suicide attempts as well as suicidal ideation. DBT is a structured approach to therapy that combines elements of cognitive behavioral therapy and mindfulness-based cognitive behavior therapy. Although DBT shows promise for use with adolescents in schools (Mazza et al., 2016), at the same time it is an approach that requires substantial training to deliver effectively and a considerable time commitment to implement.

Other data suggest that with patients in emergency care settings, one hour of psychoeducation followed by nine follow-up check-ins, either in person or by phone, significantly reduced subsequent completed suicides among patients when compared to a treatment-as-usual control group (Fleischmann et al., 2008). A similar study of over 3,000 individuals hospitalized because of suicidal ideation found that sending a supportive letter to patients four times a year for 5 years significantly reduced suicide rates (Motto & Bostrom, 2001). Although certainly not as comprehensive as DBT, follow-up check-ins by phone, in writing, or in person are a simple strategy that could be implemented easily in school settings.

Chapter 10 Takeaway Points

- Both internationally and in the United States, suicide is one of the leading causes of death among adolescents.
- Shneidman (1993) argued that unbearable psychache, or psychological pain, is an essential condition for suicide to occur.
- The interpersonal theory of suicide proposes that people die by suicide after developing two qualities: (1) a passive desire to die and (2) increased capability to kill themselves.
- The desire to die arises from a combination of thwarted belongingness and perceived burdensomeness.
- In addition to the desire to die, those who attempt suicide also develop the capacity to take action on this desire, which comes from a lowered fear of death and elevated pain tolerance.
- Warning signs are immediate signs or symptoms that indicate the desire to die and/or an increased capacity to take action on that desire.
- Risk factors are less immediate and are characteristics of persons, families, or their broader family, social or historical factors that research has shown to increase a person's vulnerability to attempting suicide.
- Immediate warning signs are (a) talking or writing about death, dying or suicide; (b) threats to kill oneself; (c) looking for ways to kill oneself; and (d) seeking access to means.
- Significant risk factors include (a) prior attempts, (b) depressive disorder, (c) substance abuse and alcohol disorder, and (d) impulsivity.
- A comprehensive assessment of suicide risk should include both warning signs and risk factors but warning signs are a first priority.
- Safety planning intervention is a useful immediate intervention that can be helpful in coping with a suicidal crisis. It includes (a) recognition of personal warning signs, (b) internal

comping strategies, (c) socialization strategies for distraction and support, (d) social contacts for assistance in resolving suicidal crisis, (e) professional contacts for assistance in resolving suicidal crisis, and (f) means restriction.

- Longer-term check-ins in person, by phone, or in writing can also be useful in helping someone who has been suicidal continue to cope.

References

Acri, M. C., Gogel, L. P., Pollock, M., & Wisdom, J. P. (2012). What adolescents need to prevent relapse after treatment for substance abuse: A comparison of youth, parent, and staff perspectives. *Journal of Child & Adolescent Substance Abuse, 21*(2), 117–129.

American Association of Suicidology. (n.d.). *Know the warning signs of suicide*. Retrieved from http://www.suicidology.org/resources/warning-signs

Centers for Disease Control and Prevention. (2016a). *Fatal injury reports*. Injury Prevention & Control: Data & Statistics (WISQARS™). Retrieved from https://www.cdc.gov/injury/wisqars/fatal_injury_reports.html

Centers for Disease Control and Prevention. (2016b). *Leading causes of death*. Injury Prevention & Control: Data & Statistics (WISQARS™). Retrieved from https://www.cdc.gov/injury/wisqars/leading_causes_death.html

Creed, T. A., Reisweber, J., & Beck, A. T. (2011). *Cognitive therapy for adolescents in school settings*. New York, NY: Guilford Press.

Durkheim, E. (1951). *Suicide: A study in sociology*. New York, NY: Free Press.

Edwards, S. J., & Sachmann, M. D. (2010). No-suicide contracts, no-suicide agreements, and no-suicide assurances: A study of their nature, utilization, perceived effectiveness, and potential to cause harm. *Crisis: The Journal of Crisis Intervention and Suicide Prevention, 31*(6), 290–302. doi:10.1027/0227-5910/a000048

Fleischmann, A., Bertolote, J. M., Wasserman, D., De Leo, D., Bolhari, J., Botega, N. J., ... Thanh, H. T. (2008). Effectiveness of brief intervention and contact for suicide attempters: a randomized controlled trial in five countries/Efficacite d'une intervention et d'un contact brefs chez les personnes ayant tente de se suicider: essai controle randomise dans cinq pays/Eficacia de una intervencion de informacion y contactos en los casos de intento de suicidio: ensayo controlado aleatorizado en cinco paises. *Bulletin of the World Health Organization, 86*(9), 703–709.

Hansen, A., Heath, M. A., Williams, M., Fox, J., Hudnall, G. A., & Bledsoe, C. (2012). No-suicide contracts with suicidal youth: Mental health professionals' perceptions and current practice. *Contemporary School Psychology, 16*, 145–159.

Joiner, T. (2015). *Why people die by suicide*. Cambridge, MA: Harvard University Press.

References

Kann, L., McManus, T., Harris, W. A., Shanklin, S. l., Flint, K. H., Hawkins, J., … Zaza, S. (2016) Youth risk behavior surveillance—United States, 2015. *Morbidity and Mortality Weekly Report, Surveillance Summary, 65*(6), 1–174.

Kleiman, E. M., Riskind, J. H., Schaefer, K. E., & Weingarden, H. (2012). The moderating role of social support on the relationship between impulsivity and suicide risk. *Crisis: The Journal of Crisis Intervention and Suicide Prevention, 33*(5), 273–279. doi:10.1027/0227-5910/a000136

Klonsky, E. D., & May, A. (2010). Rethinking impulsivity in suicide. *Suicide and Life-Threatening Behavior, 40*, 612–619.

Klonsky E. D., Qiu T., & Saffer, B. Y. (2017). Recent advances in differentiating suicide attempters from suicide ideators. *Current Opinion in Psychiatry, 30*(1), 15–20.

Linehan, M. M., Comtois, K. A., Murray, A. M., Brown, M. Z., Gallop, R. J., Heard, H. L., & Lindenboim, N. (2006). Two-year randomized controlled trial and follow-up of dialectical behavior therapy versus therapy by experts for suicidal behaviors and borderline personality disorder. *Archives of General Psychiatry, 63*, 757–766.

Linehan, M. M., Goodstein, J. L., Nielsen, S. L., & Chiles, J. A. (1983). Reasons for staying alive when you are thinking of killing yourself: The Reasons for Living Inventory. *Journal of Consulting and Clinical Psychology, 51*, 276–286.

Linehan, M. M., Korslund, K. E., Harned, M. S., Gallop, R. J., Lungu, A., Neacsiu, A. D., … Murray-Gregory, A. M. (2015). Dialectical behavior therapy for high suicide risk in individuals with borderline personality disorder: A randomized clinical trial and component analysis. *JAMA Psychiatry, 72*(5), 475–482. doi:10.1001/jamapsychiatry.2014.3039

Marshal, M. P., Dietz, L. J., Friedman, M. S., Stall, R., Smith, H. A., McGinley, J, … Brent, D. A. (2011). Suicidality and depression disparities between sexual minority and heterosexual youth: A meta-analytic review. *Journal of Adolescent Health, 49*, 115–123. doi:10.1016/j.jadohealth.2011.02.005

Mazza, J. J., Dexter-Mazza, E. T., Miller, A. L., Rathus, J. H., Murphy, H. E., & Linehan, M. M. (2016). *DBT® skills in schools: Skills training for emotional problem solving for adolescents (DBT STEPS-A)*. New York, NY: Guilford Press.

Miller, D. N. (2018). Understanding and preventing youth suicide: Ideation-to-action theories of suicidal behavior and their implications for school-based suicide prevention. In P. Terry & R. Price (Eds.), *Understanding suicide: Perspectives, risk factors and gender differences* (pp. 165–186). Hauppauge, NY: Nova Science.

Motto, J. A., & Bostrom, A. G. (2001). Follow-up for parasuicidal patients. *Psychiatric Services, 52*(9), 1254. doi:10.1176/appi.ps.52.9.1254-a

Richter, S. S., Brown, S. A., & Mott, M. A. (1991). The impact of social support and self-esteem on adolescent substance abuse treatment outcome. *Journal of Substance Abuse, 3*(4), 371–385. doi:10.1016/S0899-3289(10)80019-7

Rudd, M. D. (2008). Suicide warning signs in clinical practice. *Current Psychiatry Reports, 10*(1), 87–90.

Rudd, M. D., Berman, A. L., Joiner, T. J., Nock, M. K., Silverman, M. M., Mandrusiak, M., … Witte, T. (2006). Warning signs for suicide: Theory, research, and clinical applications. *Suicide and Life-Threatening Behavior, 36*(3), 255–262.

Rudd, M. D., Joiner, T. J., & Rajab, M. H. (2001). *Treating suicidal behavior: An effective, time-limited approach*. New York, NY: Guilford Press.

Shaffer, D., Gould, M. S., Fisher, P., Trautman, P., Moreau, D., Kleinman, M., & Flory, M. (1996). Psychiatric diagnosis in child and adolescent suicide. *Archives of General Psychiatry, 53*(4), 339–348. doi:10.1001/archpsyc.1996.01830040075012

Shea, S. C. (2009). Suicide assessment: Part 1: Uncovering suicidal intent—a sophisticated art. *Psychiatric Times, 26*(12).

Shneidman, E. S. (1993). Suicide as psychache. *The Journal of Nervous and Mental Disease, 181,* 145–147.

Skärsäter, I., Langius, A., Ågren, H., Häggström, L., & Dencker, K. (2005). Sense of coherence and social support in relation to recovery in first-episode patients with major depression: A one-year prospective study. *International Journal of Mental Health Nursing, 14*(4), 258–264. doi:10.1111/j.1440-0979.2005.00390.x

Sommers-Flanagan, J., & Sommers-Flanagan, R. (2012). *Clinical interviewing* (4th ed.). Hoboken, NJ: Wiley.

Stanley, B., Biggs, E. A., & Brown, G. K. (2014). Safety planning to prevent suicidal behavior. In S. H. Koslow, P. Ruiz, & C. B. Nemeroff (Eds.), *A concise guide to understanding suicide: Epidemiology, pathophysiology, and prevention* (pp. 366–371). New York, NY: Cambridge University Press. doi:10.1017/CBO9781139519502.041

Stanley, B., & Brown, G. K. (2012). Safety planning intervention: A brief intervention to mitigate suicide risk. *Cognitive and Behavioral Practice, 19*(2), 256–264.

Underwood, P. W. (2000). Social support: The promise and the reality. In V. H. Rice (Ed.), *Handbook of stress, coping, and health: Implications for nursing research, theory, and practice* (pp. 367–391). Thousands Oak, CA: Sage.

Van Orden, K. A., Witte, T. K., Cukrowicz, K. C., Braithwaite, S. R., Selby, E. A., & Joiner, T. J. (2010). The interpersonal theory of suicide. *Psychological Review, 117*(2), 575–600. doi:10.1037/a0018697

Whiteside, S. P., & Lynam, D. R. (2001). The five factor model and impulsivity: Using a structural model of personality to understand impulsivity. *Personality and Individual Differences, 30,* 669–689. doi:10.1016/S0191-8869(00)00064-7

World Health Organization. (2001). *The world health report, 2001: Mental health: New understanding, new hope*. Geneva, Switzerland: Author.

World Health Organization. (2014). Mental health: Global focus, local lessons. *Medicus, 9*, 21.

CHAPTER 12

Pulling It All Together and Communicating the Results of Assessment Interviews

In Chapter 1, I argued that interviewing was unique among assessment methods in providing the insider perspective necessary to obtain an authentic and credible description of a child. It is also unique in its flexibility to serve different purposes in the assessment process. Earlier chapters explored how interviewing fits into a comprehensive assessment, as well as how to structure an interview, and strategies for eliciting comprehensive and accurate information. Chapters 6 and 7 focused on the unique demands of interviewing young children and clients of diverse cultural backgrounds. Chapters 8 through 11 transitioned to interviewing for different purposes: diagnosis or classification, clarifying academic problems, strengths, and risk of self-harm.

Interviewing for assessment and interviewing in counseling or psychotherapy are different, but there are important similarities. In an assessment, the professional sets much of the agenda, and in counseling, the client has more control of the direction of the session. At the same time, it should be clear from reading the scenarios in earlier chapters that they share many similarities and that the differences are ones of degree rather than quality. This should not be surprising. Effective counseling begins with assessment, and useful assessments lead to activities or programs that help clients improve their situation in positive ways. Otherwise, as mentioned earlier, assessment is a dry technical activity that stakeholders find unproductive if not simply burdensome.

This chapter will focus on broad guidelines for understanding the different purposes of an assessment and a general structure of assessments, no matter the purpose.

Beginning: Answering the Question—Why Am I Doing This?

The primary goal of this book is to encourage students and practitioners to make greater use of interviews in assessments. Implied in this goal is another goal, which is that students and practitioners have greater confidence in their ability to gather information directly from stakeholders and more trust in the judgments they make from these data. Part of this confidence comes from having a protocol to follow that includes the kinds of questions that need to be asked for a particular purpose. An example of this is the steps to a diagnosis or classification discussed in Chapter 8. More confidence comes from knowing what the goals of an assessment are and what questions should be answered upon its completion (Hass & Carriere, 2013). In Chapter 1, I proposed that practitioners develop a focus for the interview by thinking through the goals and topics beforehand. There are, of course, several specific questions that might be answered by an assessment interview, but there are five broad paths that provide a general starting place for most situations:

1. All assessment interviews seek to understand how stakeholders perceive the problem or issue at hand, including how culture influences these perceptions.
2. All assessment interviews seek to gather information about strengths and resources.
3. Some interviews seek to clarify the nature of the problem from an outside perspective and develop a formal diagnosis or classification of the problem. This includes history and developmental information.
4. Some interviews, when the problem is explicitly academic in nature, seek to gather information about a client's direct experience with academic tasks.
5. A few interviews, where there is a threat of self-harm, will focus on understanding what underlies that threat and to what extent the client is at risk of following through.

For example, 1 through 4 would be appropriate directions for a student who is doing poorly in reading and is suspected of having a specific learning disability. For another student who was referred to a school counselor because of poor attendance, the starting place would be 1 and 2 with 3, 4, and even 5 as possibilities.

Another aspect of developing a focus for an interview is to decide with whom you need to talk. Most of the examples in this book have been with children and adolescents. This is deliberate because it often seems more difficult to interview children and adolescents than it does to interview adults. At the same time, it is important to acknowledge that a comprehensive assessment could easily involve interviews with parents and teachers, as well as students.

The Middle: Having the Conversation

In Chapter 3, we discussed the opening of an interview as consisting of introductions and small talk followed by a transitional structuring statement. The transitional structuring statement serves as a conversational marker that signals a shift in the conversation. The structuring part of the statement serves to communicate what direction the conversation is going. As discussed in Chapter 3, I recommend that the statement include asking the client for permission to continue. These opening strategies—introductions, small talk, and transitional statement—are in service of lowering anxiety and building a positive working relationship for what is to follow. What follows is a focused conversation whose goal is to gather certain information while at the same time continue the process of building a cooperative relationship. Here we return to the different foci discussed earlier. All assessments will seek to gather information about the client's perspective (e.g., student, parent, or school staff, etc.)—more specifically, their perceptions of their difficulties and the strengths and resources they can bring to bear on those difficulties. More specific information is called for when a diagnosis or classification is needed, and different strategies such as CBA or clinical interviewing are used when the focus is academic performance. Lastly, even more specific information is needed when there is threat of self-harm.

End Game: Communicating the Key Information From Interviews

No assessment is complete without communicating the results to key stakeholders. The most important of these are parents, teachers, and the clients themselves. In any assessment scenario, key findings would be communicated verbally. In some cases, often when a diagnosis or classification is needed, the results are communicated in a written report. The primary goal of communicating assessment results, whether verbally or in writing, is to provide information that is helpful to the recipients. Assessment results that are helpful positively impact the actions of those who work with a child (Hass & Carriere, 2013). This means that when we consider what to communicate to stakeholders, we must consider what aspects of the information we have gathered are most essential and helpful.

For example, for the student who is doing poorly in reading and is suspected of having a specific learning disability, we would gather information about her perceptions of school and her academic performance. We might zero in on her performance in reading using curriculum-based assessment or clinical interviewing as described in Chapter 9. In addition, we would gather information about her strengths. In the end, we would have obtained a great deal of information from interviewing alone. In addition, we would often also have information from school records, tests scores, and classroom observations. Our job in communicating assessment results is to create a cohesive narrative out of this data that responds to the concerns of the referring party and provides the most essential and helpful information.

In the following dialogue, the school psychologist is explaining the assessment results to Mrs. Hodges, who referred her 8-year-old daughter, Anna, for an evaluation because she seemed to be having difficulty in reading.

Practitioner: ***"Hi, Mrs. Hodges, thanks for taking the time to talk with me. You have to take some time off work to come in, don't you? I forget what you do." [*small talk*]***

Mrs. Hodges: ***"Sure, no problem ... I work down the street at the law office. I am a paralegal."***

Practitioner: ***"Okay, that sounds like interesting work but super busy."***

Mrs. Hodges: ***"Yeah, sometimes, but I also have some flexibility."***

Practitioner: ***"Oh, good. Again, thanks for coming in. You know that at your request we have been doing an evaluation of Anna. When we first talked, you thought she was doing well socially and doing pretty well in math but you were worried about reading. Does that sound about right?"***

Mrs. Hodges: ***"Yes ... I just don't understand. She does so well in so many other things but she just struggles with reading."***

Practitioner: ***"Yes, I can understand. Well, as part of the assessment, we did several things. One is that I read with her and we talked about what it was like for her to read. We also did some reading tests, but I wanted to start with my observations from talking with her. Would that be okay?" [*overview of assessment process and transitional statement*]***

Mrs. Hodges: ***"Sure, she doesn't say too much to me about it when I ask."***

Practitioner: ***"Well, when I talked with her, she said she really likes math and when she showed me some of the math she was working on, it seems she is right in there with the rest of her class. I was especially impressed that when I read some word problems to her, she seemed to really enjoy figuring them out. She also said that she liked social studies and science, both of which are pretty hands-on in her class so she seems to like be active and working with others. [*key information but note that the practitioner starts with strengths*]***

Mrs. Hodges: ***"Okay, that is good to hear."***

Practitioner: ***"When we talked about reading, she said that she actually likes stories but feels like she reads slowly and it takes her a long time to figure out how to sound out the words she doesn't know quickly. When I had her read from a third grade text, it did seem like she read slowly and spent a long time trying to figure out how to read words she didn't know right away. When I told her some words, which meant she could move along more quickly, she seemed to understand what she was reading just fine. When I let her struggle through things, she didn't always seem to get what she was reading. So, it seems the issue is figuring out how to speed her reading up a bit so she can take in what she is reading."***

Mrs. Hodges: ***"What do you recommend? I just don't want to her to start hating school."***

Practitioner: ***"Given she is doing so well in so many things, I want to make sure we keep her with her classmates as much as possible. I have two ideas. One is that her teacher meets with kids after school for extra help. I talked with her and she said that she would be glad to work with Anna. Also, we have a reading specialist who works with kids three times a week for about 45 minutes. Anna would be with four or five other students about her age. She would miss a little in science or social studies, but I think we can figure that out. Also, we will do that for about eight weeks and see how things are going then. How does that sound?"***

Mrs. Hodges: ***"That sounds great ... when would she start?"***

Practitioner: ***"Next week if that is okay with you. Also, we'll plan to meet in November to talk about how she is doing. Feel free to send me a message if you have any questions in the meantime. Also, let me know what Anna thinks of the group after she starts."***

Mrs. Hodges: ***"Thanks, I will."***

What were the essential points communicated in this conversation? First, Anna is doing well in math and enjoys social studies and science. More specifically, she seems to enjoy those subjects because they are taught in a hands-on manner that allows her to be actively engaged in learning with others. Next, although she seems to comprehend what she reads, she is slow to read words and her decoding is deliberate and lacks the automaticity needed to read smoothly. Additional key points, especially important to Mrs. Hodges, include the goal of any proposed intervention ("So, it seems the issue is figuring out how to speed her reading up a bit so she can take in what she is reading.") and what changes in Anna's educational program could be implemented to reach those goals (extra help from teacher and assistance from the reading specialist). It is also important to note that this information was communicated in a way that was respectful, making it more likely that the relationship continued to be collaborative.

As previously noted, some situations call for a more formal written presentation of assessment results. In schools, this most often takes place when there is need of a comprehensive evaluation that examines if a student has a disability per IDEIA. This is a high-stakes decision that demands not only a comprehensive assessment but a clear, well-written report of those findings. These two aspects of an evaluation cannot be separated; a poorly written report can obscure the value of a well-done assessment, but a well-written report cannot rescue a poorly executed evaluation (Hass & Carriere, 2013). Practitioners often seem more comfortable writing about scores than about interviews. This may be because it seems more objective to state that a student earned a standard score of 59 on a test and that score represents below-average performance for his age than to describe how the same child described his depression or anxiety.

Following is an excerpt from a report that has information from both a mental status observation and an interview. Note that this is only one excerpt from a longer report that describes a comprehensive assessment focused on several questions, including "How does Arturo function socially and emotionally?" and "What special education classification would be most appropriate for Arturo?"

During the assessment, Arturo was cooperative but gave up very easily when test items were difficult. He rarely smiled and gave brief answers to questions. When asked to elaborate on an answer he often said, "I don't know." Arturo seemed irritable and sullen during both the administration of tests and conversation.

When interviewed, Arturo said he is "always getting mad" and often got into trouble for arguing with his teachers or with classmates on the playground. Arturo said he was "trying to be good" but that sometimes the teachers were mean to him and his classmates "bugged him." When asked why he thought this happened, he responded, "I don't know" and was unable to provide any further details, despite several prompts and follow-up questions.

When asked about friends, Arturo could name several boys he regarded as friends. He said he enjoys riding his bike with them and being outdoors. When at home, Arturo said he likes to watch sports on TV. He also reported that he belongs to two soccer teams and a track and field club. For soccer, he plays games most Saturdays and Sundays and practices Mondays, Tuesdays, and Fridays. He goes to his track and field club on Wednesdays.

Arturo's teacher, Mrs. Johnson, described Arturo as social and popular with other students. She also noted that he can seem "on edge" and "stressed." Mrs. Johnson also reported that Arturo often fidgets and picks at things such as paper or erasers anxiously. She also said that although Arturo is not physically aggressive, he can be oppositional and will "dig in his heels" when he does not want to do something. Mrs. Johnson said that on the playground, Arturo gets into trouble regularly for being disrespectful to staff. She believes that this seems to happen more with female staff than male staff.

As discussed earlier, all assessment interviews seek to understand how stakeholders perceive the problem or issue at hand and try to gather information about strengths and resources. Some interviews seek to clarify the nature of the problem in such a way as to formulate a formal diagnosis or classification of the problem. In this case, someone who read this report would know something about how Arturo understands the problem (although he did not have a lot to say about this) and something about his strengths, for example, he seems to have friends and enjoys sports. Of course, there is not enough information here to make a diagnosis, but the excerpt communicates that there was useful information obtained from the interview, for example, he seems "on edge and stressed," he seems to be oppositional, he fidgets and picks at things, and he seemed irritable and sullen. Given other information, this might lead to a classification of ADHD or depression or both.

A second excerpt follows. This is also from a larger report of an assessment of Johnny, a 16-year-old high school student. Johnny was referred because he was not making adequate progress toward graduation despite special education.

When interviewed, Johnny was cooperative and answered questions willingly. Although he was cooperative, Johnny's affect was restricted and his mood seemed negative. He said that his classes were easy but admitted he does not always try. Johnny said that in his free time he likes to play the guitar, draw, watch moves, and read. He reported that he likes to "hang out with friends" at lunch, but other than this, Johnny did not mention any specific friends or group activities he enjoys. When he was asked to describe his typical day, his descriptions of his activities were him doing things alone, and he did not mention interacting with anyone at home or school.

Johnny's primary special education teacher, Mrs. Kennedy, was also interviewed as part of this assessment. She described Johnny as a "sweet kid." She said that he has few friends but tends to move from group to group at break or lunch, having interactions that she believes are superficial. She also believes that he seems to do better socially with adults.

In Johnny's case, a reader would know that Johnny believes the work is too easy, but he not is motivated to do it. This may or may not be true objectively, but it does offer the insider perspective. Readers would also know something about his interests and potential strengths. We know that his teacher views him as "sweet," suggesting he can interact positively with adults. We also know that he seems to have difficulty interacting with peers. The interview information is certainly not enough to come to any certain conclusions about Johnny, but what information it does provide is stated clearly enough that it can be linked with data from other assessment methods. In other words, if we discover that Johnny's academic skills are low, we can assume that his remarks about his work being too easy are probably defensive. If an assessment of his social skills suggests he is lacking in the social skills needed to interact appropriately with his peers, this would help us understand why he finds it easier to interact with adults, who often offer more scaffolding for conversations with youth than their peers.

Chapter 12 Takeaway Points

- All assessment interviews seek to understand how stakeholders perceive the problem or issue at hand, including how culture influences these perceptions.
- All assessment interviews seek to gather information about strengths and resources.
- Some interviews seek to clarify the nature of the problem from an outside perspective and develop a formal diagnosis or classification of the problem. This includes history and developmental information.
- Some interviews, when the problem is explicitly academic in nature, seek to gather information about a client's direct experience with academic tasks.
- A few interviews, where there is a threat of self-harm, will focus on understanding what underlies that threat and to what extent the client is at risk of following through.
- Communicating the results of an interview, either orally or in writing, is a critical step in a comprehensive assessment.

References

Hass, M., & Carriere, J. A. (2013). *Writing useful, accessible, and legally defensible psychoeducational reports*. Hoboken, NJ: Wiley.

APPENDIX 1

Child and Adolescent Interview Protocol

Child's name: ______________________________

Interviewer's name: ___________________________

Date of interview: ____________________________

Home/family

1. Whom do you live with? (If there is a noncustodial parent, find out what the visitation schedule is.)
2. Family living outside the home?

Health

3. Recent doctors' visits?
4. Significant illnesses or injuries?
5. Medication? Now or in past?
6. Vision and hearing?

Education/school

7. Current school? Grade or level?
8. School history, including preschool?

9. Favorite classes or subjects?
10. Most difficult classes or subjects?
11. Do you get any extra help with these subjects? Who helps you? How do they help you?
12. Recent grades?
13. Experiences with homework? (How does the student experience homework? Is it difficult, easy, and so forth?) About how much homework does the student complete in a day or week? (Try to get a percentage.)

Activities and self: Positive qualities, interests, and skills and engagement in productive activities

14. What are some things you like to do or think that you are good at?
15. How do you like to spend your free time? What are ways you have of relaxing and having fun? Hobbies? Sports? Music/movies?
16. How do you relax and have fun with your family (including common interests and activities)?

Coping

17. How do you calm yourself down when upset or angry?
18. How do you handle difficult or stressful situations? Give an example of the last difficult situation you faced and how you handled it.

Social support and role models

19. What are your friends like (ages, gender)? What are some things you like to do together?
20. Who are you closest to in your family?
21. When you get into trouble at home, how do your parents handle it?
22. Who in your life helps you reach your goals or explore your interests?
23. Name some people that you respect or that you see doing things you like or appreciate. What kinds of things do they do?

Required helpfulness

24. Who counts on you? [Follow up with, What do you do for them?]
25. Tell me about a time you did something nice for someone else, or you helped someone out, or you gave the person something he or she needed. What types of things do you enjoy doing for others?
26. How do you help out around the house?

Participation in community

27. Do you belong to any clubs, teams, community organizations, or churches (synagogues, temples, or some such)?

Goals and aspirations

28. If things went well for you over the next month, what would be different?
29. How do you see yourself in a year?
30. How about when you are an adult?

Transitions

31. Did you recently change schools or are you planning to change schools?
32. Have you changed houses or are you planning to move soon?
33. Have there been any big changes in your family recently?

"Waking day" interview

34. Think of a regular day for you. Tell me what you do first thing when you get up? Next? And then what … (have child describe what he or she does from waking up to going to bed at night).

Screening for problems

35. Have you been feeling sad or angry lately? (D)
36. Have you lost interest in or stopped enjoying the things that you usually like to do? (D)
37. Have you ever thought your life was not worth living or thought about hurting yourself in some way? (D)
38. How is your appetite? What kinds of things do you like to eat? Have you gained or lost weight lately? (D)
39. How do you sleep? About how much do you sleep each night? (D)
40. Do you often have trouble paying attention to details or keeping your mind on what you are doing? (ADHD)
41. Are you told to sit still a lot? (ADHD)
42. Do you usually get upset and lose your temper if things don't go your way? (ODD)

43. Do you talk back or argue with your parents a lot? Your teachers? (ODD)
44. Do you worry more than other kids your age? (if yes) Do you worry as often as every day or every other day? What do you worry about? (A)

Summary sheet/global impressions

45. Significant strengths
46. Significant needs/risks
47. Actions needed to enhance strengths and reduce risk

APPENDIX 2

Questions About Language and Culture

1. What language did the client learn first?
2. Ask client what language he or she uses when speaking to:
   - Parents
   - Siblings
   - Others in household
   - Adults in the neighborhood
   - Peers in the neighborhood
   - Adults at school
3. Ask client what language he or she prefers when:
   - Listening to music
   - Watching TV
   - Reading at home
4. Client's educational experiences:
   - Years of education in home language
   - Years of bilingual education
   - Years of English-only education
5. Information about parents:
   - Time in United States
   - Parents' occupations
   - Parents' level of education
   - What language does the client believe he or she speaks best?

APPENDIX 3

Process of Deferential Diagnosis

What symptoms or behaviors are of concern?	Are these behaviors typical or atypical?	What is the most accurate and fairest classification of the problem?
	Are these behaviors typical or atypical for the client's development? What is the weight or extent of the symptoms and problem behaviors? 1. How long have they lasted? 2. How often do they occur? 3. In what settings do they occur? 4. How long do they last? Impairment—How do the symptoms and behaviors impact the client's life? 1. Phenomenological impairment—distress 2. Impact on peer relationships 3. Impact on adult relationships 4. Impact on academic achievement	Are the problems developmental? that is, did they begin early in development? Are the problems primarily internalizing, externalizing, or a mix? 1. Are the client's problems primarily internalizing or externalizing? 2. If mostly internalizing, is distress or fear the primary issue? 3. If mostly externalizing, are the behaviors more oppositional or conduct? 4. Are there signs of a thought disorder? What diagnosis best fits the information? 1. What are the most likely possibilities? 2. Of these, which one seems the most likely given the evidence?

APPENDIX 4

School-Based Mental Status Evaluation

Student name: ______________________ DOB: ______________________

Examiner: ______________________ Date: ______________________

Mental Status Observation of Social Emotional Functioning

Affect (What emotional state best describes how the student looks now?)

____

____

____

____

____

____

Mood (How does the student describe his or her emotional state over time?)

____

____

____

____

____

____

Social skills during interview: eye contact, turn taking, reaction to praise, and so on

____

____

____

____

____

____

Description of friends and activities

____

____

____

____

____

____

Appearance	**Speech**
Wears glasses ____________	*Appropriate speed and volume for age and development* ____________
Hearing aids ____________	Seems overly fast or slow ____________
Appropriate dress and grooming ____________	____________
Seems healthy ____________	Too loud or soft ____________
Height and weight for age ____________	Amount ____________
Disheveled ____________	Articulation ____________
Clothing is dirty ____________	Conversational proficiency ____________
Unusual physical characteristics ____________	____________
Appears sick or unhealthy ____________	____________

Posture *Relaxed, appropriate to situation* __________ Slumped __________ Rigid or tense __________	**Decision-Making and Judgment** *Seems appropriate for age and development* __________ Seems impulsive __________ Seems unusually reflective or slow to act __________
Body Movement and Attention *Normal for age and development* __________ Overactive for age and development __________ Agitated __________ Slowed __________ Attention to tasks __________ __________	**Thought Content** *Appears normal for age and development* __________ Obsessions/compulsions __________ __________ Delusions __________ Suicidal ideation __________ Fears __________
Attitude Cooperative __________ Friendly __________ Controlling __________ Dependent __________ Hostile, challenging __________ Guarded, suspicious __________	**Perception** *No unusual perceptions noted* __________ Illusions __________ Auditory hallucinations __________ Visual hallucinations __________

Mental Status Notes __________

Author Index

F

G

H

Subject Index

R

S

Y

Printed in the USA
CPSIA information can be obtained
at www.ICGtesting.com
LVHW060358051224
797844LV00005B/101
9781119166863